Goodbye Mary Lou

Scott T. Sammis

Contents

Chapter 1. "The Terror"

A low rumble high up ahead strikes terror deep into our hearts. The sun has just risen above the peak of Mount Kilimanjaro and is burning our faces at 9:45 in the morning. Bright blue sky above, no clouds. "How could something bad happen here in this incredibly beautiful, sacred place?" I wonder, confused. We are so close to the top. Local Tanzanians call the mountain "Big Mama." The rumble turns into a growl, as if Big Mama is angry, or maybe waking up on the wrong side of the bed. My whole family, Mary 57, Trevor 25, Becky 22 and John 20, is here on the Western Breach of Kilimanjaro at 17,000 feet elevation. Intense foreboding explodes in my chest. "This cannot be good," my brain gasps.

The first boulder begins to cascade down the Breach to our right. So far up ahead, it seems small and slow. It tumbles, bouncing up and down, breaking many other rocks, sending them scuttling in every direction. Trek leader Kambona yells "Don't move! Sit down!" He has big responsibilities to the 13 remaining climbers and the 75 porters ahead of us. A proud Masai, he feels no panic, for he is strong. But we are in deep trouble. Now the rock has grown as big as a Volkswagen beetle and is hurtling by us at blinding speed, hell-bent down the Breach. I watch in awe, standing, thinking "Wow, this is like a National Geographic special on rock slides, only we are in the middle of it." It seems surreal. "I'm going to witness something few people ever get to see."

That naïve thought vanishes in the next second. A wave of smaller rocks shoots past us on the left. Disbelief and wonder turn to sheer panic. If the rocks are on our right and left, that means we are dead center. "Welcome to the killing field. Danger is here on Big Mama," I realize. These boulders start small up ahead and get BIG fast. My brain can't imagine how fast. The only analogy my addled brain can draw is to the game Dodge ball we used to play in elementary school. It was easy to evade, at the very last moment, the soft rubber balls thrown by my 10 year old classmates. "These rocks are much faster and lethal," I tell myself, "If you want to have any shot to survive, buddy, you gotta dodge far ahead of the boulder's approach." Kambona is down on one knee, still yelling "Get down!" Mary and the children are down. Becky has ducked her head, but now raises it. She decides she must see what is coming. Trevor and John are prone, heads up. I am still standing, perched precariously on the loose rock of the Western Breach of Mount Kilimanjaro, waiting, awestruck.

Mary Lou is my wife of 28 years, my best friend, confidant, soul mate, and spiritual leader of my family. Earlier this day, at 5am, she stirred in the dark to the sweet sound of the gentle wake up call from our porter "Good mahning, good mahning." As we climbed the last week, Mary has struggled mightily, suffering through nausea, vomiting, diarrhea, depletion, and depression. She has lost ten pounds, and her beautiful freckled face, framed by strawberry blond hair, is pale and gaunt. Kambona is anxious to get the group moving by 6am up the Breach. We don't know what the hurry is, but we see his anxiety. Mary is up, dons five layers of clothing, gloves, hat and gaiters, and moves to the mess tent where she tries valiantly to choke down tea and toast. She is waiting at the staging area at 5:45am. "I'm ready," she says, "we can do this." She grabs the first spot in the hiker line that will snake up the steep, unstable mountain behind assistant trek leader Amassa. She smells the finish line, like a thoroughbred. "I want this," she says, as the line starts to wind its way slowly up the Breach. "Polay, polay," say the porters as they pass, in their sing-song way, "Slowly, Slowly." Mary is putting one foot down, resting to breathe the thin air - only about half as rich as at sea level - placing her poles again, and finding the next foot placement on the loose gravel. "Step, breathe, step, breathe." When the rocks come, Mary is facing down the mountain, catching her breath, drinking water, and removing a layer or two of clothing. She is exhausted. Kambona yells "Sit down!," but Mary is already sitting, facing away from the terror that is coming.

Betty Sapp, Wade's wife and an accomplished Appalachian Mountain hiker, was wearing a heavy Irish knit sweater and no hat when the climb commenced. It was well below freezing, biting cold and dark, three hours before sunrise. She was last in our hiker conga line, just before Kambona. At 9:30am it is Betty who calls out, "I'm hot, can we stop to take off a layer?" The peak of Big Mama, looming ahead of us, has blocked the sun until now, delaying the "sunrise." The brilliant sunlight has almost a physical impact on us, quickly roasting our faces and raising our body temperatures rapidly. In the sunlight, we can see more clearly the rivulets of water melting off the ice trickling down the rocks along the path.

Mount Kilimanjaro at 17000 feet in January is normally covered by snow and ice, locked in solid. The trek leaders routinely chop foot holds for the hikers that are following. This year's loose rock surface is very unusual. As our porters hustle by us carrying the huge duffels of gear on their heads, to the final summit camp, Kambona yells to them "Don't knock rocks! It will start a slide!" He has worried that we started too late. Had we launched at 6:00am as he begged us to do, we would have been across the Breach by now, safely. Reluctantly, Kambona agrees to break. "Stop, drink water, change clothes. 15 minutes, no more." Betty is standing when the rocks come. Mary's poles are on the ground. I am grateful for the stop. My head is pounding with a persistent four day headache, and it has taken all my focus this morning to lift my next foot forward. I look down the mountain in the bright glare. There are pinpricks of light, like tiny diamonds, in my field of vision. "I hope we make it to the top before the Acute Mountain Sickness hits me and they have to stick me in the hyperbaric chamber. If that did happen, at least my physical misery would be over. That would be a blessing," I muse to myself. AMS has been on my mind since we started.

Now the rocks are flying right at the heart of the group, missiles fired by an angry mountain. At the back of the hikers line, Kambona watches one of the early rocks hit Betty. The rock slams her in the forehead, knocks her back, bounces off and comes at the head of Kambona. He dodges. Three more come for him, two small and one big. Trevor is on his belly yelling "On your right! On your left! Rock! Rock!" Becky does what she was told to do, ducking her head, but then makes herself look up to avoid being whacked. Ironically she is immediately stung on the chin by a flying fragment, drawing blood. Still, she "can't not watch." Trevor remembers the bouncing and breaking rocks creating "the worst fucking sound in the world." Rocks the size of garbage cans are whipping through the group. So FAST. We are sitting ducks. Trevor escapes the barrage. John is struck on the wrist, lucky not to break a bone.

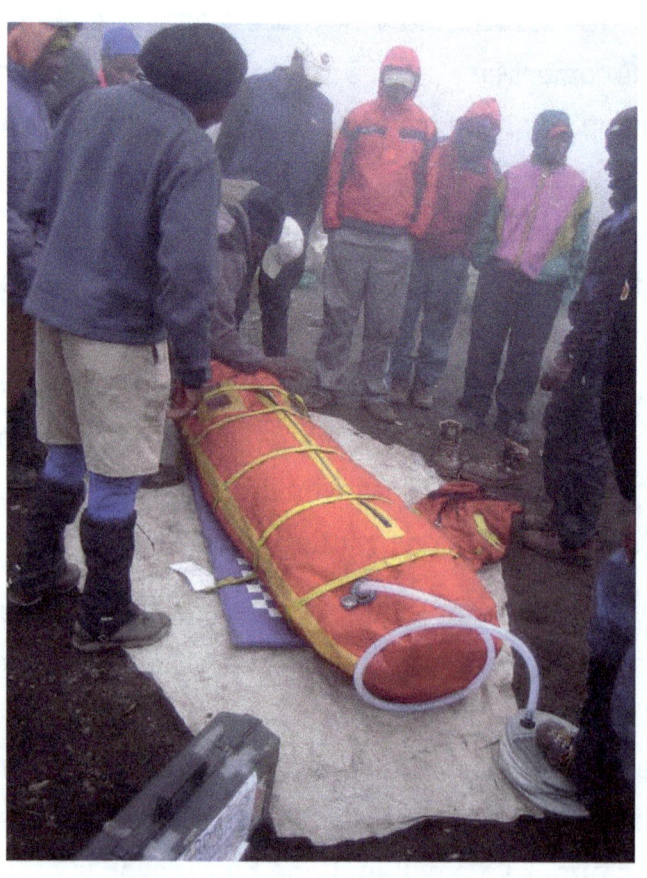

The battle is on. Standing, teetering tenuously on the steep slope, I either ignore or don't hear Kambona's instructions to get down. I'm thinking "there's a good chance I can die, here on Kilimanjaro. But I can't leave my sweet Mary Lou or the children. I must survive this." There it is, the bullet with my name on it. Hurtling right at me, expanding insanely from pea-size to softball to basketball in the blink of an eye. It is now or never. This evil death rock wants to take me away from Mary and the kids! NO! I start the dodge early, lurching to my right, twisting my left shoulder back, trying to present a narrower target. The bastard, grown now to the size of a small garbage can, misses me by inches. I can feel its cold breath on my face as it passes. "Holy mother of God, that was close!" Now I'm on full alert, ready for the next one. I know in my heart that Death is here, on the Western Breach.

Just as suddenly as they started, the rocks stop coming. The sun is still bright, but the last few moments seem dark in my memory. Kambona says later there were 200-300 rocks in the bombardment. There is quiet. I have survived. Hah! I need to make sure my family made it. Must take a personal inventory of the four souls who are the closest to my heart. I look to my right. Betty is on her back, in her Irish knit sweater, splayed out on the scree, unmoving. Her head took a direct hit. It looks to me like she was blown backwards by the force of the blow, leaving a trail of blood in her wake. My son John says to his brother Trevor, "We gotta help Betty!" Trevor says quietly, "Man, she's fucking dead." I don't hear this

7

conversation at the time, but in my inventory-taking I note, with massive relief, that Trevor is standing and OK. Thank God. Becky is up. Hallelujah. John is OK. Whew. Where is Mary? Up in front, I remember. I see she's down! My heart sinks.

My Mary is passed out, her head in John's lap. I watch in abject disbelief. This can't be happening. Right after Mary was struck, Amassa cradled her, then gave way to John, so he could go get help. There was no blood, no obvious injury, just Mary's beautiful face contorted in pain, struggling to stay with us. Trevor comes up and whacks her hiking boot with his, imploring her "Get up! Wake up!" John gives her mouth to mouth resuscitation, yelling "Stay awake, stay awake!" She regains consciousness but is still groggy, sleepy, out of it. Amassa comes back and hears or sees something in Mary. "Jesus Christ," he exclaims. Hearing this Becky realizes her mom's condition is serious. John feels it too, and is suddenly overwhelmed. Becky takes over, holding Mary's head and torso in her lap. "Mom, where are you?" Mary replies sleepily "on a mountain."

"Good," Becky thinks, relieved momentarily. "It hurts, it hurts," Mary cries, wincing in some as yet unrevealed pain. Becky asks "is it worse pain than childbirth, Mom?" Mary smiles through the pain, "No. You are the best daughter." Kambona is here with oxygen for Mary. Becky gives way. "Bye, Mom. I love you."

Meanwhile Kambona has been performing his own

inventory of the carnage on the killing field. Having barely escaped the clutches of death himself, he needs to triage the situation. He sees Betty bleeding from her ears, eyes, and mouth, and knows she can not be helped. He goes to Paul Cunha, our guide from the Appalachian Mountain Club, who was hit in the head and shoulder and is bleeding on the ground. "Do you know what happened?" he asks Paul. "No," comes the foggy reply. Kambona instructs Carol, Paul's wife, to hold gauze firmly on his head wound to stop the bleeding. That head wound could kill him. Tajiri, one of the porters, has 100 open wounds on his leg. Kambona tourniquets the leg to stop the bleeding and uses poles to set it. "His bones were falling out on the ground," Kambona later recalled. Tajiri will lose the leg to amputation. Next, Mary. She is conscious when he arrives the first time, complaining about pain in her right arm and difficulty breathing. Right away he hears a fluid in her lungs and a gurgling sound. Amassa whispers to Kambona, "pulmonary edema?" "No," says Kambona, in case the nearby children can hear. "Mary is OK." He suspects a rib break and lung puncture which would explain the tortured breathing. In his heart he knows she won't survive long. Kambona calls for oxygen, unsure it will help, and continues on his triage rounds.

Kambona finds Virginia de Lima and Jack Foresteire, the two single hikers, to be unhurt. Virginia points to Wade, whose wife Betty is motionless, lifeless, gone. Bill and Lucy McCord, a wonderful couple from New Jersey, are with Wade, who is able only to stare down the mountain, stunned. "I have candy," Wade offers, eyes glassy, not making coherent sense out of the scene before him. The rocks didn't hit Wade, but the enormity of his loss has. He is reeling, lost within himself, just breathing, not feeling. Paul is responding well; his head wound is not life-threatening, but his shoulder is ruined, broken in so many places he will require years of therapy. Kambona runs back up to Mary, who is now in Becky's arms. "Ask questions, Becky, Get answers." He listens again for the gurgling in her chest, which confirms the lung puncture. Oxygen will not help. He knows when the oxygen leaves the lung through the puncture hole it bubbles and causes severe pain. Mary cries "give me the oxygen!", then pushes it away. She is drowning, up here 17000 feet above sea level, but the cure hurts far worse.

When I realize my poor beloved Mary Lou is hurt I wrest myself from my unsteady foothold, fall several times on my way to her, sending more rocks cascading, and scramble to within 6 feet of her. Her head is back, eyes closed. Not knowing what else to do, I take a photograph of Mary. Why did I do that? There are people all around her. I don't want to interfere, don't want to impede her treatment. I don't approach any closer. I will wonder why for the rest of my life. I am close enough to hear her complain about her sore right arm. Her face is etched in pain. I convince myself she has a badly broken arm. I decide they will carry her down below 15000 feet and a helicopter will whisk her away to an emergency hospital. Up here at 17,000 feet the air is too thin for the choppers to operate. In a few days we can take her home to recuperate and tell stories. It dawns on me our trip is over and we can finally escape this terrible mountain. The thought warms me, relieves my headache for an instant. What doesn't occur to me is my wonderful wife, Mary Lou, the beautiful force of nature, is mortally wounded. Even when Kambona gently lifts the back of Mary's clothing layers to reveal lacerations and bruises on the right side of her back, I don't get it. I see no blood, but the marks tell the story of a severe blow. Mount Kilimanjaro is claiming the love of my life, my soul mate, my Mary Lou, and I'm clueless.

It is time for Mary to be carried off the mountain. Kambona directs six porters to place Mary gently on the large duffel they have cut to make a makeshift tarp. They lift her so carefully and then smoothly hustle her down the mountain. I don't have a chance to touch her, kiss her, wish her good luck or tell her "I love you," like I have one million times before. I would tell her I love her when she went to the grocery store, for God's sake. It happens fast. I cling to my helicopter fantasy. "She'll be OK. We're going home."

John, the youngest, is taking charge, acting like the patriarch in this, the worst crisis of our lives. He will accompany the porters carrying his mother.

Trevor is also coming up big. He asks John "You got this (going down with Mary)? You got her? You need my help?" "No thanks, I got this," John says. They both agree "Dad's leg is bad.

He needs help." Trevor will stay behind and make sure I make it down safely. John scampers down the mountain ahead of the rescue party carrying Mary. How he keeps his balance I will never understand. Maybe it's all those years skateboarding and surfing.

After taking care of her mom like a champ, Becky follows the rescue party with Amassa, Virginia and another porter. Amassa is in radio contact with Kambona and the expedition headquarters. "We are all broken," Becky hears Amassa say into the radio. "Are you joking?" comes the office reply. Kambona's voice crackles, "No, we are serious. We have one dead and one not doing good." Silence on the radio. Becky is alarmed. She peppers Amassa with questions: "Is she conscious? Is she alive?" "I don't know" comes the answer. As the rest of the porters pass, they look sadly at Becky and say again "Polay, polay." Only this time it means "Sorry, sorry."

Chapter 2. "The News"

Events have gone terribly, horribly wrong on Mount Kilimanjaro. What was supposed to be an exciting family adventure has turned into our worst nightmare. The family is splintered, information is scarce, fears are mounting, and beautiful Mary Lou's life is swinging in the balance. With her youngest, John, running ahead, she is being transported as gently as possible by six strong young Tanzanians down the steep, loose rock field called the Western Breach. Her right lung is filling up with blood, her breathing is more and more labored and painful. She struggles to remain conscious. She knows she must fight to stay with her beloved kids and husband and extended family, but a peace beckons just beyond the darkness of her closed eyelids. The makeshift duffel tarp shifts under her as the six brave tarp-bearers struggle to keep their balance, keep up the pace.

At one point the radio crackles: it is Amassa saying "I think she is dead.' Kambona scolds "No think, you must know." His stern tone makes Amassa reconsider, "I think she's alive." The headquarters tries to relieve the tension: "Don't fight." Trying to protect the children, who he believes are close to Amassa, Kambona gives instructions: "Make the kids not see. Don't stop. Keep them busy." He knows Trevor and his I are lagging well behind, out of earshot, and blissfully ignorant.

John has been watching like a hawk the six porters carrying his mom, searching for a sign. He reaches Arrow Glacier Camp first, consumed with doubt and dread. He races back up to meet the porters and sees his mom's eyes are rolled up in her head. Frantically John badgers the head of the tarp-bearers, Sigfried, for the answer he already knows. "Is she alive? Is she alive? IS SHE ALIVE?" Sigfried has been told by Kambona to protect the children, as was Amassa, so he hesitates. Finally he shakes his head sadly, watching John's face dissolve. The enormity of the truth crushes the brave 20 year old. He sobs bitterly. Numbly he follows the porters back down to Arrow Glacier Camp. Now they have become pallbearers.

Becky picks her way down the Western Breach, hoping against hope, trying to make sense of Amassa's cryptic radio chatter. She too asks Amassa about Mary's status. After Sigfried confirms her death to John, Amassa calls Kambona and relays the message "Mary is dead." Searching Amassa's face desperately, she finally gets the answer she dreads more than anything. Becky's beloved mom, her best friend, confidant and heart connection, is gone. She falls apart, knees buckling, eyes spilling over, wailing from the blow. Virginia and the porters comfort her and eventually, gently, get her moving again, down to Arrow Glacier Camp. When they reach camp, John is waiting, and they hug and weep inconsolably. The worst possible thing in the world has just happened. It's real. And "Dad's still up on the mountain with Trev. They don't know," they realize. They want to wait and tell us, but Kambona makes sure they keep moving. His mission is to get the living off this unstable mountain before another slide or Acute Mountain Sickness or an emotional breakdown cause more of his charges to be carried off by the tarp-bearers.

Our quiet, steady porter Nelson has drawn the job of shepherding Wade and me, the two husbands of the stricken women, and Trevor down the treacherous Western Breach after the rock slide disaster. There is still danger of another slide, but I know Kambona is concerned about Wade's mental and psychological state and my possible AMS. My leg hurts so bad that Nelson takes my backpack. He now carries front and back. I am slowing down the group, but nobody seems to mind. Everyone else has left the mountain and is ahead of us. We are the last four. Nelson has no radio so we have lost contact with the others. Trevor asks how I'm doing. "My head still hurts, and the leg is slowing me down. I can't wait to get off this infernal mountain and see Mom. I hope she's OK," I reply hopefully. "I'm sure she is," Trevor says. I cling to the helicopter fantasy, rejecting the possibility Mary could actually die from back bruises and a broken arm. Of course the doubt keeps pinging all of us. Nelson turns to be sure we are all making progress down the dangerous mountain. Slow, plodding, deliberate progress.

Arrow Glacier Camp is abandoned by the time we get there. We push on to a "coffee camp", where tents are set up for tea and biscuits. A few moments earlier, bigger groups of porters had gathered to carry Mary, Paul and Tajiri out faster. 22 strong backs were mustered, and they set off ahead. We sipped some tea amid an eerie silence. The sunny conditions on the upper mountain had given way to the soupy gray fog of mid-day. Engulfed by the unwelcome cold clouds, I began to succumb to feelings of depression. We sleepwalked through Lava Tower Camp on toward Shira 2 Camp and the takeout road where jeeps awaited. Trevor asked again how I was. "Can't wait to get out of this hell hole. Things will be better tomorrow." Trevor was a trooper, keeping a steady pace. Wade just looked off into the distance and kept walking.

It was late afternoon when Kambona caught up to us. I had been calculating how much faster we were going downhill versus uphill the past few days. Perhaps twice as fast, even at the snail's pace I could manage. My head still pounded with each step, but the ache was becoming bearable. Maybe it was the thickening air. Kambona stood in front of us, solemn. To Trevor and me he said "It was a terrible accident. There was a lot of injured people. I'm really sorry. I have something to tell you. I'm sorry. Mary also is dead." Trevor cried out "Oh, no, that can't be possible!" I merely shook my head, never so stunned in all my life. Astonishment briefly gave way to defiance. Mary gone? Completely unacceptable. Trevor collapsed to his knees sobbing, Wade began to cry. I wailed "No, no, no, no!" What will I do? Life without Mary? It was unthinkable, a concept too immense to accept. I grabbed up

Trevor, and Wade joined us in a standing, weeping embrace. Nelson and Kambona put their arms around us. Wade pulled away first. He was a few hours farther ahead of us in the empty, lonely territory we are just entering. Kambona remembers Trevor crying extensively, but not me. "No cry, very strong, very strong," he told me later. I believe he spun that memory for my benefit. I recall crying until I gasped for breath, completely bereft and hopeless.

Now the walking took on a whole new tone – it had become a death march. Step by leaden step. As we emerged from the cold, gray mid-day cloud, the sun and mist brightened some, even as our mental state filled with darkness. I was in a stupor. My knees hurt, my head still throbbed, and my heart was shattered. I wanted only one thing: to get to John and Becky and hug them for all my life. My future was a black hole, unfathomable, incomprehensible. Besides gathering my splintered family in my arms, my soul needed only "to get the hell off this mountain. Now."

Kambona predicted we would reach Shira 2 Camp, one of our stops on the way up Kilimanjaro, in about an hour, and we did. We walked through camp like spirits floating through a ghost town. I was sensing we were close to seeing Becky and John, which consumed me at the moment. "So much has been taken from me today, let me please just have the chance to feel my children in my arms again," I implored. I asked Nelson, who was still carrying my backpack seven hours later, "was it far to the trailhead?" "No, not far," came his reply. Ten minutes, twenty, thirty, forty agonizing minutes passed by as my bitterness and consternation mounted. At the 50 minute mark, the trucks and brightly colored jackets appeared in the distance and my body eased. There they were! John and Becky ran up the trail toward us. We four dissolved into tears together. Just to touch them, feel them sobbing, shuddering beneath the enormous weight of our loss brought solace to my soul. My desperation ebbed. I looked at them, "you OK?" They nodded. Becky was bleeding from a chin cut, John from a wrist bruise. Their eyes were red and wet, but bright and relieved. We turned toward the group below, perhaps 50 people, including porters, our remaining hikers, some folks from the Colorado group behind us on the Western Breach who also lost a climber, and drivers. Waiting for the arrival of the two widowers and the bereaved eldest son must have been brutal for all of them. Somber isn't a good enough word to describe the mood that day.

Kambona suggested we form a circle to honor the three dead climbers, Mary, Betty and Christian, from the Colorado group. We all backed up and linked arms. All eyes drifted to me, so I choked out how wonderful and warm and full of life Mary was. Touching all three kids, I told a story: "Any one stick can easily be broken, but a bundle of sticks cannot . Our family is like that bundle of sticks. We will survive this." Wade said some kind and thoughtful words, as did a woman from the Colorado climbers. When no one else spoke, an awkward silence fell upon us, just as the sun set. It was strangely touching. I realized later most of the participants, porters mostly, spoke only Swahili, so they weren't going to speak or understand much. I also wasn't aware until later that Mary's body was 75 feet away in one of the trucks. Kambona's touch, I'm sure, to keep us ignorant and safe. I worried about our duffels – all but Becky's had been abandoned in the rapid exodus off the Western Breach. Kambona said "Mahmood has been assigned to stay at Arrow Glacier to collect and return all the bags." What he didn't say was that Betty would remain on the mountain for two more days, before they were able to bring her down the Western Breach of Mount Kilimanjaro.

We now placed ourselves in the complete care of African Environments, our travel expediter extraordinaire. Dazed, empty, exhausted and determined only to stay close to each other, we allowed ourselves to be hustled into a well-worn Landrover. The "takeout" road provided a bouncy, jolting, back-breaking ride. "How long to the hotel?" one of us asked. "Two and one half hours," came the reply from our driver. I secretly hoped that estimate wasn't based on Nelson time. We were joined along the rutted trail by another friendly guide who had been part of the evacuation team that got Paul and Carol out to the hospital to begin repairs on his ruined shoulder. He bought us bottled water at the Park Entrance gate. It was there we signed out of Kilimanjaro National Park in the harsh glare of a single bare light bulb, watched wordlessly by a machine-gun toting uniformed guard. Eerie.

The ten-foot tall "Points to Remember" warning sign Becky and I had photographed lightheartedly a week earlier on the way into the Park faded slowly in the rear-view mirror.

The dreamlike journey down from the takeout position to the Moivaro Coffee Plantation Guest Houses ended with a warm welcome by African Environments partners Wes and Mellie Krause and Richard Beatty. They could not have been more helpful, concerned or sympathetic. They soothingly told us "everything will be arranged, all bureaucratic red tape handled by us. Please just relax. There will be medical attention and grief counselors here tomorrow. A special dinner is being prepared for you in the dining hall." Before dinner and bed I knew I needed to complete one chore: call home.

There was no available landline phone service that evening, but the internet was up, albeit intermittent. The BBC was reporting already that three climbers had been killed in their tents at base camp by an avalanche. I knew I needed to call home to pass on the devastating news, but also to clear up the BBC's misreporting. My first call was to my father Quentin and stepmother Marge at their home in Florida. No answer. It was late afternoon Wednesday, January 4, 2006. They were probably doing errands. "I have some bad news," I messaged with a massive lump in my throat, "there has been an accident on Kilimanjaro. I'll call you again soon." I hated leaving a message like that. My next call was to my partner

Frank. I called him at work, in a different location than my dad. He answered right away, "Hey buddy, what's up?" I knew this was going to be brutal, "Before you hear it on the news or see it on the internet, there's been an accident. We got caught in a rockslide near the top of Kilimanjaro, and Mary was hit. She died shortly after." Frank gasped loud enough for me to hear it eight thousand miles away, shattered "Oh my God, Scott, oh my God!" I choked up, my throat closed up momentarily, as it hit me again. "The rest of us are OK, a little banged up," I croaked, "I couldn't get through to Quentin. Would you try? All I have is a borrowed satellite phone." I promised to email details and a request to get the arrangements started back home. "Scott, I feel so sorry. I know how much you loved Mary. Oh my God. Don't worry, I'll take care of everything. Get the kids home safely, buddy," he signed off. I did reach my dad in the next half hour. Marge was devastated, sobbing uncontrollably, wailing in the background. My dad was calm, already thinking of what needed to be done.

In the few quiet moments I had after I hung up the satellite phone, pacing the grounds of the Moivaro Plantation, my brain was suffused with thoughts of home and my marriage journey with Mary Lou . Maybe my mind needed some happy memories as an antidote to the terror of the current moment. My thoughts drifted to a much pleasanter time, when I first met and married the vivacious Mary Lou Salzman from "San Mateo, California."

Chapter 3. "The Beginning"

The handwritten note about the upcoming Hampton Hawes jazz concert in Half Moon Bay appeared, out of thin air, on my desk. I'd only been out here in California a few months but I knew Half Moon Bay was down the coast some from our office of Industrial Indemnity Insurance Company in downtown San Francisco. The note, attached to two tickets, read "Mary Lou Salzman, 10th floor, would like to know if you're interested in going." The note was unsigned. Hmmmm. "Who sent this?" I wondered. Was it the trickster Joy, our department yenta? Mary's vivacious buddy Joan Johnson? My pal and future best man Steve? I knew about the light-hearted, sassy, radiant, blond, freckle-faced beauty from ogling her across the lunch room at Industrial Indemnity. It was 1975. I was 23, barely on my feet in San Francisco, living in a studio apartment with a Murphy bed, making $750.00 a month. Quite a catch, I reckoned. I waited the appropriate few hours - didn't want to appear too anxious - then showed up at her desk holding the note and tickets. "Hi Mary Lou, I'm Scott," I offered, not sure she knew who I was, "do you know anything about these?" She smiled coyly, gesturing to take the pieces of paper, "no, let me see." I waited while she looked them over, then asked "I'm free, can you make it that day?" Looking a little dubious, but incredibly cute, she smiled "let me check my schedule. I'll get back to you."

Turns out Mary was available. I offered to drive my company car, a Chevy Vega, but she insisted on picking me up and going together in her dilapidated green VW bug. I learned later she always drove herself to first dates, providing her plenty of escape routes out of bad situations. Chivalrous me, I brought a squat bottle of Mateus rose wine. We talked easily as the VW cruised the spectacular coastline on Route 1. Soon we were seated in the small auditorium. As the venerable jazz saxophonist made his way on stage, I looked over to smile at Mary. Her head was back, mouth already pulling on the Mateus bottle like a thirsty pirate. "Wow," I thought, "this could be a fun first date." After two lively sets, Hampton announced he would break protocol, and "seeing as how y'all are such a cool audience, I will come out for a third set." Well, the audience erupted in gleeful applause. I turned to Mary, expectantly. She was sound asleep, slumped in her seat. Needless to say, we missed the third set.

I steered my beautiful, inebriated first date back to the vintage VW, belted her in, and began the drive north to San Francisco. She was awake, but a little sheepish when we pulled in, headfirst into a tilted parking spot near my Victorian apartment on broad Baker Street in the Haight/Ashbury district. Hoping she would come in to sober up with a cup of coffee, I opened the driver's door, walked around back, and reached for the passenger side door handle.

By the time I got there, Mary had already hopped over the gearshift, no mean task in that tiny car, and was planted in the driver's seat, looking straight ahead. "Hmmmm," I thought, "no coffee. Maybe I can at least get a good night kiss." I walked back around and leaned in the driver's window, hoping for a peck on the cheek. The little VW engine revved up, the car shot backward instantly, and I nearly lost my nose. Mary didn't even wave as she sped off down Baker Street. "Well, so much for that date," I ruminated ruefully, "and I thought it was going so smoothly. Really great girl, can't hold her liquor, and not interested in me. Oh well."

For the first time in countless numbers, I misread Mary Lou. She called a few days later to apologize and explain her bad date escape routine. "Was the date that bad?" I wanted to know. "No, silly, I was mortified at getting drunk. You made me nervous." We agreed to try again, minus the alcohol this time. As the weeks passed and we fell hopelessly in love, we kept teasing each other. It would go like this: "Are you free Friday night?" "No, how about Saturday?" "I'm not good Saturday, how about Sunday?" "Oh, wait, I just remembered, Friday night is OK. What time?" We'd wind up spending the entire weekend together. Neither one asked about how the other's schedule magically cleared up. I had been dating actively the previous year, and Mary's romantic pattern was a triangle: one past lover hanging around in the wings, a current "for now" boyfriend who was OK, and a prospective partner hovering in the landing pattern. My dating ceased abruptly, Mary's backlog and landing pattern cleared, and we realized we were head over heels in love. "Who's kidding who?," Mary would say. I remember telling her "I'm only available for you on days that end in Y."

Meeting Mary's folks was fun for me. Harvey was garrulous and energetic, Amy quieter and more intense. Harve liked me from the get-go, but "he likes everybody," Mary would say. Amy was a tougher sale. She was a rough critic of her husband, reminding him constantly that he talked too much. It was clear to all that I was crazy over Mary, and as the days passed I would catch Amy smiling at me. As we left her house one day Amy gave me a big hug and said "Well, I'm glad Mary finally found her prince. She had to kiss a lot of frogs, you know!" "Mom!" Mary protested. When we eventually got married and I carried their sweet Mary Lou away 3,000 miles east to Boston, I thought their hearts would break. I found out much later they couldn't have been happier. They knew I would be good to Mary and take care of her, and they would see her often.

I was off to Harvard Business School's first semester in the fall of 1976 and we were not engaged, but I left my cat Stutz so she knew I was commited and coming back. I flew back to San Francisco the first weekend I could get off in October to ask her to marry me and go ring shopping. Her folks were thrilled, but we didn't tell mine until Christmas. Mary flew to Boston to meet me for yhe holiday, and we drove down Route 95 to Long Island, New York together. My mother, Ellie, was the tougher of my parents also, and I had told Mary some of the stories of her strict German-Swiss upbringing and character. Without realizing, I scared Mary so much she started to brush her hair to get ready to meet Ellie a little early – in New Haven, two hours early! Ellie and Quentin fell in love with Mary instantly. I proposed, on my knees, at the Mill Pond Inn in Centerport. "I promise to love you and take care of you forever," I said. We both cried. The future seemed blindingly bright.

We chose the church we wanted to be married in not by denomination but by fenestration. The church we selected in Portola Valley had a magnificent stained glass A-framed wall facing gorgeous redwood trees. The minister needed to interview us to assess our suitability as marriage partners. We had barely seated ourselves in his office when the pastor asked us both "What is your personal relationship to Jesus?" I could feel Mary tensing. She'd had some frightening religious experiences in her grandfather's Pentacostal church. She'd been "saved" one time too many at the altar of what she called her granddad's "jumping and shouting" church. When the Jesus question popped up, she punted, "Scott, why don't you handle that one?" I had to think for a moment, but then confessed "I've never really met Jesus personally, so I don't have a personal relationship. I like some of his ideas, like the Golden Rule, and try to live by them." I'm not sure the good reverend much appreciated my answer. At the end of the session he summed up his evaluation, "You two obviously love each other very much. One thing to be careful of is your tendency to cover up your true emotions with humor." Hmmmm. We couldn't wait to get married.

The wedding at the magnificent Portola Valley stained glass cathedral, surrounded by stately redwoods, was the perfect start to our marriage journey. I knew I would love Mary Lou forever. I just wanted to take care of her. "Do you promise to love her, honor her, be faithful to her, in sickness and in health, until Death do you part?" Yes, Yes, Yes. And Mary took care of me every day of our marriage. 28 and a half years later it seemed she was still caring for me and the kids even after Death parted us.......

TL - (B) Chris' wife, Terri, Mary, Virginia, Delores, Amy, (F) Shirley, Sally, Trevor, John; TR - Ashley, Mary, Sonja
BL - Harvey, Mary, Amy; BM - (B) Shirl, Amy, Mary, (F) Steve, Sally; Yosemite

Chapter 4. "Revelation"

Midnight at the Moivaro Coffee Plantation near Arusha, Tanzania found the remaining Kilimanjaro climbers, now down to nine, gathered around the dinner table lit by candles in the dark. The air was cloying, the mood somber, all nine of us having difficulty finding words. The day's tragedy hung on us like a heavy blanket. Usually there would be a light banter, but humor didn't even occur to us. Vegetarian fare for my children, chicken or pork for the rest, all served with such care in the stunned silence. I remember the pumpkin soup. It was delicious, but I recall not having much of an appetite. Wade, Trevor, Becky, John and I would stay for a few days until arrangements could be made. Bill and Lucy would head home to New Jersey tomorrow, as well as Virginia to Connecticut and Jack to Massachusetts. I'm sure they made valiant attempts to comfort us, and I'm sure we appreciated them. The four of us were dreading the quiet hours to come in the rest of our night...

Before dinner Richard Beatty gathered Wade and me to discuss what needed to happen with Betty and Mary. He patiently explained the egregious bureaucratic labyrinth that would need to be negotiated in order to have their bodiescleared to return to the U.S. They would need to be inspected, autopsied, tested, checked and triple checked by a variety of security organizations, before being released for transfer back to the states.

Richard estimated the process could take the better part of a week. He gently offered another, local option which offered elegance, simplicity and would take less than half the time: cremation. Richard described a gracious two day ceremony to be presented by a Hindu group located in the midst of bustling Arusha. The group had been providing cremations here for over 130 years. Wade calmly and quickly opted for cremation. "This is clearly Betty's choice," he stated without hesitation. Richard seemed slightly pleased. They both looked at me. "Mary would have loved this. Her essence can stay here where it was released. We will get her ashes to take with us, right?" I asked. Richard was gracious, "of course." He paused for a moment to consider, "I believe this will be the first double cremation of two women in the group's history. Thank you both. It's a lovely ceremony and you will be on your way home in three or four days, as opposed to a week or more. We will take care of everything. Please rest assured."

In due time dinner was over. We said our goodnights and began the slow walk to our cabins for the night. Warm air, dim lights. We were vaguely aware of flowers and dense foliage swaying softly in the breeze. Really we just placed one foot in front of the other. The keys to cabins #2, 3,and 4 dangled from big wooden paddles, probably to be sure we didn't take them home in our duffels by mistake. Cabins 3 and 4 were adjoining triples so we chose them. Flipping on the light we saw mosquito netting, rope moldings, and a warm rustic look. The occasional spider or gecko skittered away from the light. We hardly noticed. This was their home, we were the strangers.

We brushed our teeth and took showers, chatting to keep away the thought of what was coming. "Can you find your toothpaste? Here, have some of mine." "Where the hell is my contact lens case? Do you have a spare, Dad?"

Soon, we slipped into our beds, and Becky was sobbing right away. John joined her under the netting for a hug and to add his tears. Trevor and I pushed our beds close so we could all touch and sob. "Oh my God, how could this have happened to us? How can Mary not be here with us? How will we get through this night, the next morning, and the rest of our lives?" We would have cried all night had not sheer exhaustion pulled us into a deep sleep.

I awoke to the sounds of Becky sobbing softly at 6am. We all gathered again to touch each other and ward off the yawning, enveloping loneliness. As the sniffles subsided I asked "Beck, are you OK?" "Yes, but I don't know how I'll get through this day," she said softly. We sleepwalked through morning ablutions and shuffled out onto the grounds of Moivaro. The plantation was transformed by the morning light. Now the bougainvilla-festooned, verdant foliage created a peaceful, restful feeling. Just a handful of other trekkers and friendly African staff were around. It seemed a perfect setting for our particular passion play. Kambona and Amassa met us and shepherded us to breakfast. The familiar omelets, granola, pastries and coffee gave us hope maybe the world wasn't coming to an end.

The medical staff of two Tanzanian doctors and a Scottish nurse practitioner attended to John, Becky, Jack and Lucy. Jack got a full head dressing, Becky received an obtrusive, oversized yellow bandage with big letters ARG on it. I gave her a smaller bandaid from my first aid kit to replace it. John refused a bandage for his wrist cut, but I kissed his booboo and he smiled.

Robin, the grief counselor, came to us, and I volunteered to go first. She was a lovely, spiritual lady with deep pool eyes and great wisdom. A strong Catholic, she nonetheless affirmed my reliance on rationality to cope with these disasters. "Without a rigid rule set to explain the difficult things that happen ('God wanted Mary with Him' for example), rationality admits mysteries, and is tolerant that answers may not come until a later date, or never," she explained patiently. Sensing my guilt for having lead the family on this ultimately disastrous adventure, Robin pointed out "you chose a vacation with risks, but you minimized them by selecting African Environments and AMC to guide you." The incredible care we were receiving made me see the truth in that statement. Nobody was to blame. The rock slide was a random event. Bad luck for Mary and Betty and the injured, and for us. "I am worried sick that Mary suffered badly in the minutes before she died," I offered. "I know you are," Robin said," but let me remind you that Mary suffered worse pain – childbirth – three times." Wow, I thought, remembering the 18 hour labor Mary endured birthing Trevor, our first. The fetal contraction monitor on Mary's abdomen would flat line at the top of the range for what seemed like an eternity as my new wife bravely suffered yet another killer contraction, one of many. My heart bled for my poor Mary Lou that night. I was so touched by Robin's ministrations and the peace they brought me that I all but begged my kids to see her. Expecting resistance, I oversold her, but they quickly agreed. All three spoke freely, cried repeatedly, and reached some level of comfort.

During that first day after Mary died, Trevor, Becky and John played endless games of "Last Card," which is similar to UNO but with a standard deck of cards, while I completed a descriptive email on yesterday's events to Frank and Mickey Clement, Mary's best friend and author, who I asked to begin memorial preparations. I wanted to dispel the BBC misinformation and begin to relieve the confusion and pain at home with facts. This email apparently spread like wild fire, eventually forming the basis of most of the ensuing news stories around the world. After I sent the email, the hotel's internet connection was lost for two days. I was glad to get it out. It was all I could do.

Kambona and Amassa stuck to the kids like glue. They called the card game "Lasty Card." There are wild cards and arcane rules which seemed to me to be subject to change depending on the circumstances of the rule giver. Whenever Amassa got stuck with the Joker (must take five cards - bad luck) he would smile broadly and say "I am so happy. I have more cards to win with." Trevor would grimace when Kambona would issue yet another clarification to a gray area situation. The five of them played another simple bluffing, bidding game called "Bullshit." Kambona lied fairly well about what cards he did not have in his hand, as did my offspring. Amassa was much more transparent and easy to detect. When caught bluffing and forced to take a fistful of cards back into his hand, he would smile that goofy grin and say again "I am so happy. More cards to win with!" Becky and John goaded their two new best friends with "You cheater!" constantly, to which Kambona would protest in mock seriousness and Amassa would feign great indignation. The five of them laughed the day away, happy to divert themselves from the lurking emptiness and heartbreak. It is truly wonderful how close relationships are forged in the crucible of emotional crisis.

Lucy and Bill, Virginia and Jack left at 5pm to catch the 9:45pm KLM flight 689 to Amsterdam and home. We all tearfully hugged and promised to stay in touch. They drove off in the van, waving. Now we were down to five original climbers. Wade and the four Sammises tromped off on a nature trail tour of the plantation grounds: fantastic banana and coffee plants on an immaculately groomed trail. Wade's spirits were remarkably high, I thought. An engineer by trade, his rational discipline was barely holding on in the battle with his fears and emotions. "I'm sorting out Betty's things little by little, deciding which to take home, which to donate, which to discard," he said calmly. Wade teared up a lot on the trail, but never broke. He and Betty were childless, so I figured the loss of his best friend had to be excruciating. The five of us hugged a lot. I wondered if my children were dreading the sorting of Mary's belongings as much as I was....

The KLM airplane that took Lucy, Bill, Virginia and Jack back to Amsterdam brought Pam Hess down from AMC to be with us. She seemed to be everywhere, comforting us, thinking of every contingency, and in constant contact with Heidi Reilly, our guardian angel back at AMC Headquarters in Boston, Massachusetts. I swear Heidi did not sleep for 48 to 60 hours straight after Mary's death. She was ground control, information central, and dispatcher all in one, also in charge of responding to USA relatives and the insistent media, among other things. Pam was generous with her time and her heart, and she eventually gravitated to Wade's side. We four had each other.

Darkness came to Moivaro Plantation and to our hearts. Dinner with Pam, Wade, Kambona and Amassa was a mixture of somber small talk and good natured jabbing about the card-playing atrocities of the day. Kambona and the kids valiantly tried to keep the mood light, but I knew we four were dreading the night ahead of us, the quiet, desperate hours, the yawning black abyss. We were all still so raw, so utterly stunned to the core. After dinner we once again sleepwalked back to Cabins 3 and 4, the keys dangling from the big wooden paddles. We brushed teeth, removed contacts and dropped, one by one, into our netting shrouded beds. Soon the muffled sobs and sniffles started. John comforted Becky and I joined immediately. Trevor followed, but he had been toughing it out all day. He rationalized, at the advanced age of 25, "grief is so self-centered." He had been studying Zen to help him deal with upsetting thoughts. "I've been out of the house for several years, so it's not like I can't breathe on my own," he explained. That sentiment got us thinking a different way. Soon the crying gave way to gentle jokes, laughter, sighs, and shortly the regular breathing of fitful sleep.

At 4 am I arose to visit the bathroom in the dark. All was quiet. As I settled back into my bed to let sleep recapture me, the clearest, strongest message came to me. I did not see a face or hear a voice, exactly, but the words formed in my mind and were etched into my consciousness. The message went, " I just realized I have lived the life I imagined. I have three perfect children I love with all my heart. I adore you as my soul mate. I couldn't love my sisters and brothers more. I have the best friends anyone could want. I have the money, time and freedom to enjoy them. I now realize how fleeting our time on earth is and how easily lost. I am happy for the time I had, and I will watch over you and await you. In the meantime, do not waste your time. Go, now, and live the life you imagine. I love you."

As I furiously scribbled down the message, I began to sob, not from sadness this time, but from joy. John and Becky were alarmed and came over to hug and comfort me, Trevor soon after. I read back the message to them. They broke out in tears of joy too. Their mom was here, embracing us, taking care of us, cajoling us. We knew what we had to do. In the pitch black of the Tanzanian night, lights were flipped on, duffel bags thrown open, and the sorting begun. Vast reserves of energy and goodwill were unleashed on the previously dreaded task of emptying Mary's duffel. "OK, this needs to go to the porters, this is garbage, anyone want this?" we called out. We joked and laughed and organized the mass of clothing and supplies, including our own duffels. By 6:15 the job was finished. We looked at each other, smiling but tired and relieved. The sun was up. Mary had energized us, focused us, and carried us over a big emotional hurdle. Wow, it was time for breakfast.

I have often puzzled over how this message came to me. There was no visible Mary or audible voice, just that clear idea that focused itself into my brain. I had been wrestling the last two nights in my semi-awake stake, vacillating between empty despair and a shocking giddy optimism about new purpose, new relationships, new connections. WHAM, the message came all of a sudden, and I had to jump out of bed and commit this little revelation to paper. As I wrote I choked on the beauty of it. When I finished I simply sobbed for joy. Wonderful, beautiful, warm Mary Lou Salzman Sammis from Shoreview, San Mateo, California, unpretentious daughter of hard-working, salt-of-the-earth parents, was leading us out of despair and into lives of purpose. Incredible. This quiet, twitchy, over-concerned , under-organized worry wart was boldly leading our way out of the most devastating disaster imaginable. What a spectacular legacy. I find myself so grateful Mary is still taking care of us, even after Death parted us. And I can't stop thinking of growing up with her in our early marriage......

Chapter 5. "Growing Up With Mary: Our First Marriage"

I remember the giddiness of waking up with the radiant Mary Lou in the early years of our marriage. I felt a guilty pleasure, as if we were "getting away with something." Away from our parents' puritanical eye, but possessing the full sanction of society's blessing on our marriage, we still felt deliciously naughty, making love like lusty little rabbits in every bed we could find. Through the shocking three foot snowstorm that shut down Boston in the winter of '77-78, through my angst at surviving Harvard B School's 2nd year, through scraping together enough quarters out of the couch in our tiny apartment to afford one simple dinner out each week, we didn't care. We had each other. We felt rich, bullet-proof. "Together we can handle everything and anything," we thought. Ah, the exuberance, the overconfidence of young love.

First house, first child, first crisis. At the beginning of the real estate boom of the late 70's on Long Island, New York we borrowed a $5000 downpayment, took out a $49,000 mortgage, and purchased a 20' X 30' ramshackle house on a postage stamp lot. 12 Stony Hollow Road was actually pieced together from two separate Connecticut houses transported in pieces by barge across Long Island Sound; it's twelve windows were a dozen different sizes. We decorated on a shoestring. Our firstborn was coming in January 1980. Mary quit her $12000/year job at the American Cancer Society just before Trevor arrived. His tiny arm was stretched over his head in the birth canal so Mary's painful and emotional labor was elongated to 18 hours. We sat with miraculous Trevor on the only couch in our house and pondered "how will we take care of this utterly dependent, defenseless little person and pay this gargantuan $400/month mortgage on only Scott's salary?" We cried and cried.

Ever resilient Mary rose to the challenge. She elicited advice from every corner, especially calm and competent mom Amy and mother-in-law Ellie. I got a meagre raise and took a promotion/transfer to manage the Materials/Shipping department of Allen Group Inc.'s Fajardo, Puerto Rico factory. It would mean uprooting the family from Centerport, Long Island to Puerto Rico in June of 1980. Mary accepted the challenge enthusiastically. "It will be an adventure!" she smiled brightly. Our anticipation grew throughout the spring, preparations were made to rent 12 Stony Hollow and ship our clothes, some furniture and our ancient white Toyota Corolla "Flash" to Fajardo. I was down in P.R. several weeks early, while Mary stayed back home making final moving arrangements, when our gauzy plans of sunshine and palm trees started to go off the rail.

Playing left field for the factory fast pitch softball team, I saw a sinking line drive come quickly toward me. Attempting to snag it before it hit the ground, I lurched forward on my right foot. POP! The ankle let go and I rolled over like a beached whale in left field. With my teammates surrounding me I watched as one lifted my leg and tested the ankle – my foot flopped around like a dead fish. There was no pain at that point but that unhinged foot sure didn't look good. A teammate drove me to the local backwater hospital where the crackerjack staff made me wait 2.5 hours, finally X-rayed the leg, and pronounced that it was a "sprained ankle," treatable with Epson salts and rest. Hobbling back to my apartment, unable to push off the right foot at all, I knew it was much worse than a sprained ankle. The next morning I drove myself, left-footed in Flash, to the big city hospital in San Juan. The doc said "you have suffered a ruptured right Achilles tendon. If we don't repair it immediately the tendon will crawl up your calf and you will never walk correctly again." I signed up for the surgery the next day, but, on the left-footed drive home, I pondered a week in a hospital alone, trying to decipher the doctors' and nurses' discussions with my rudimentary Spanish. I flew home to New York instead. Recuperating at my parents' house in a hip cast, we got the news about Mary's beloved dad, Harve.

Happy-go-lucky, garrulous, hale and hearty Harve Salzman had just finished a slice of his favorite lemon pie ("Oh man, I'm so full, that pie ruined my appetite!") when he felt some discomfort, pushed back from the dinner table, and died of a massive heart attack. The news hit Mary Lou like a sledge hammer. Harve always worked two or three jobs to make ends meet for his family of six children, but somehow found time to read a story to Mary before bed when he came home from work. On Friday nights, the Salzman house was full of extra kids. Harve's job was to put his six to bed. Often, as he attempted to put the sixth kid to bed, it would be a neighbor kid who would protest: "but Mr. Salzman, I don't live here!" Dog tired, Harve would say "Hush up and get in the bed. I need sleep." Busy as he was, Mary was convinced Harve loved her more than the others. Now, suddenly, her rock, her corner man, was gone. With a six month old infant and a husband on crutches in a hip cast, Mary sucked it up and made arrangements to fly to California for her dad's funeral. Through my own painkillers I remember marveling at her tenacity, wondering, "where does she get the strength?" Flying back east on United Airlines, Harvey's employer for nearly half a century, I held her hand and said "I love you. Are you OK?" She teared up. Having just lost her beloved dad, facing the task of making a home out of an apartment in a foreign country and caring for an infant and a hobbled husband, with no family or friends within 1500 miles, Mary's immediate future awaited her in Puerto Rico. I could tell she was gearing up for a tougher row to hoe than she ever imagined.

Between three trips to visit me in P.R. before we moved there, and two trips to California, tiny Trevor logged 20,000 air miles in his first 12 months. The smiley tow head seemed to adapt well to the breezy warmth of our small apartment on the 28th floor of a building in Fajardo, but at 18 months old he abruptly started to lose weight and lost all interest in food and water. His weight quickly fell from 18 to 15 pounds. Both Mary and I panicked. "Please God," I bargained, " let this beautiful baby survive. Take me if you must, just let him live." The same local hospital that misdiagnosed my Achilles rupture suggested we place baby Trevor in a room, shared with 2 older men, with an IV in his little arm. Horrified, we found a doctor in San Juan who prescribed a suppository which calmed down Trevor's bowel and allowed him to keep water down. After he stabilized and began to put weight back on, Mary told me, sternly "I can't go through that again. We have to get out of here." She was right. When we became pregnant with our daughter Becky that next spring, I knew it was time to head back north.

There were bright, heartwarming times, also. Mary yearned for her family in California, so she travelled cross country several times each year. I knew she loved VW beetles, particularly red convertibles, and was always looking for a used one. During one of her sojourns west I located an old yellow bug, had it rapidly painted cherry red, and parked it at the airport with a huge "For Sale" sign in the window with our phone number on it. As I walked her past the newly painted beauty, I saw her eye catch it. "Ooh, it's for sale! Can we look? It's perfect! Oh my God!" As she inspected the bug, her eyes fell on the phone number on the sign, and confusion clouded her baby blues. A huge smile crept over her beautiful face and she leapt into my arms, crying for joy, "I love you SO much. No one could EVER take care of me like you. Now give me the keys and throw away that damned sign! NOBODY'S buying this car away from me!"

Mary often left on her California trips very frustrated with her East Coast life, and me, but she returned singing a different tune. As our third baby John arrived in December

1984, to join two year old Becky and five year old Trevor, and we moved into our third house, the strains started to show. She began to have doubts about the real reason her mom, Amy, failed to come out East for the birth of any of her three babies. Her sisters were having babies 3,000 miles away and Mary began to feel each and every mile of the separating distance. Resentment grew that I was too involved in building a business with my father and doing too much community service. I refused to attend night meetings or play golf, so I could spend nights and weekends at home, but Mary still felt I should have shouldered a bigger part of the child-rearing load. She immersed herself completely in the task of managing the lives of our three little ones, ever attentive to each mood swing and schoolyard crisis. We arranged for au pairs to come from Denmark as mother's helpers, but Mary was so concerned about their psychological well-being that she worried over them like a fourth child, multiplying her angst. Each of us began to feel more and more abandoned by our partner, angry, yet powerless. The storm clouds gathered.

Why does this pattern of drift and alienation occur so frequently in young marriages? It is so clear to see in retrospect, so inscrutable to those in the throes, yet so impossible to warn about. Every disappointment, every argument lost, every point conceded without discussion seems to be converted into a virtual brick, which is then invisibly placed in a solid wall of resentment, dividing the couple emotionally. Soon the resentment barrier is so high and so obvious, both can feel it's presence, but neither can find a way over or around it. The bullet-proof love of the ages of which they were both so confident in the early years turns out to be instead a fragile seedling which needs constant attention and nurturing. Why is it this wisdom only arrives after a marriage has dissolved, or never at all? I think of sweet Mary Lou's urgent message of revelation for her family in Arusha, and her impending cremation and release into the universe......

Chapter 6. "Cremation"

After Mary's amazing revelation and exhortation the second night after she passed on Mt. Kilimanjaro, the four remaining Sammises began Friday January 6th in Tanzania with surprising energy, spirit and purpose. While Kambona and Amassa herded us around the teeming streets of the capital city Arusha, Richard and Wes were moving bureaucratic mountains. Many questions persisted: "Were the Police finished their investigation? The Registrar? The Coroner? The Medical Examiner? The Embassy? Could we complete the cremation later today and make the Saturday 9:45pm KLM flight to Amsterdam?" Richard advised us "there is room on the Saturday evening flight, but we would have to plump for seats on Sunday." That raised the prospect of sending the children ahead alone and me coming home with Mary's ashes by myself a few days later. I couldn't conceive of letting them out of my arms' reach, so I ruled out that plan.

We scored some unforgettable purchases in the marketplaces of Arusha. Kambona found for the kids three pairs of Masai-style sandals, made principally of motorcycle tires, similar to the ones he wore. I bought two carved wooden statues, one of two lovers embracing, another of a family tree, depicting several generations standing on the shoulders of the one below. The second one reminded me of the 1997 slave movie <u>Amistad</u>, in which defense lawyer John Quincy Adams asked the chief slave Cinque "are you afraid of losing the trial and being put to death?" "No," said the dignified slave solemnly, "I shall call upon my ancestors to help me and they <u>must</u> come, for right now <u>I</u> am the only reason they ever existed." Mary will be joining the newest level of ancestors, upon whose shoulders Trevor, Becky, and John and their children will stand. What a legacy and message she leaves them. They can be proud. Our last purchase was a tee shirt that made Amassa giggle. In white block letters on royal blue it said "MZUNGU." Kambona explained it meant "white people." We bought four. Mary would have chuckled.

Richard Beatty met us at the Arusha Hotel fresh from moving mountains to obtain death certificates and paving the way for the cremation ceremony to begin this afternoon. I believe he is a miracle worker, but I also believe the Tanzanians in all levels of the bureaucracy were touched by our story and found it in their hearts to move our papers to the top of their respective piles. I am deeply grateful. The venerable Hindu priest and his "businessman committee," a group of local merchants who facilitate the cremations, were prepared for us to arrive at 3:30pm. We showed up by bus at the enclosed compound at 6pm. The neighborhood seemed seedy and nasty but the compound was neat and well-organized, an oasis of sanity in the bustling chaos of the center of Arusha. I wondered to myself "How different was Arusha when these gentle Hindus created this place in the 1870's?"

Within the eight foot tall walls of the protected compound, there was an open, raised structure framed by a peaked metal roof. Inside the building we found Mary and Betty lying peacefully side by side on the pyre, shrouded in cream colored cloth except for their faces. The pyre was built of logs stacked neatly beneath them. Their eyes were closed, and they seemed tranquil. Looking more closely, however, their faces were pale and marked by discoloring bruises. As much as my tears betrayed my heartache, it was a comforting confirmation to see Mary's beautiful face again, if only for a few moments. Through the tears I sent her all my love once again. The Hindu priest, attired in traditional garb, quickly took charge of the proceedings. He instructed us, in a sing song voice, to adorn Mary's lips with mint oil and her body with red and white powders, flowers and necklaces, all in preparation for the journey ahead of her. He chanted and we prayed with him. Becky was unable to partake in the ceremony, so intense were her sobs. Robin, the grief counselor, and Pam from AMC wrapped their arms around Becky, but she was utterly inconsolable.

As disconsolate as Becky was, Trevor, John and I found a measure of comfort in the carefully choreographed movements, helping to prepare our beloved Mary for the next places her spirit would visit. The Hindu ceremony placed our lives here on earth in a much larger context, lessening the finality of Mary's death. Trevor and John and I continued the rote ministrations as instructed, as did Wade for Betty, placing items and walking while the priest gently chanted. The walking and completing the simple tasks distracted us from the stark reality of Mary's lifeless body lying a few feet away. Soon, however, it was time to back away from the pyre and from Mary. We were asked retire to the perimeter of the open funeral structure to watch the committee finish building the pyre. Perhaps it was the covering of Mary and Betty with logs, knowing we would never see them again, that brought on the tsunami of tears. The four of us clotted together, holding on for dear life, wracked with sobs, weeping as one. I never felt so utterly bereft and hopeless in my entire life, especially feeling the trembling bodies of my three broken children and their emptiness at losing their best friend and mom. "It simply cannot get worse than this," I realized.

When the careful placement of the logs and fire sticks was complete, tradition dictated that the youngest son, John, and the husband, Wade, be summoned up to light the pyre. Accessing some deep well of duty or respect or honor, John brushed his tears aside, purposefully took the lit wand, and touched it to the pyre. Becky could not watch, poor, wretched soul. Soon the flames were leaping 20 feet or more into the Tanzanian sunset, giant orange tongues flapping, flying, yelling into the cosmos, announcing the beginning of Mary's and Betty's journey to the next place. So majestic and powerful was the eruption of energy that we stopped sobbing, mesmerized by the spectacle and force that were lifting Mary and Betty, setting them free. I was aware of Mary's presence. She was smiling brightly, her radiance undiminished, eyes sparkling. "I love this beautiful 'hoogla boogla' ceremony. It is exactly what I wanted. Thank you," she said.

Many believe the spot on earth where our pre-human ancestors first made the leap to humanity was right here in the Rift Valley of East Africa, where Mary's ashes were now rising into the warm Tanzanian night air. The theory is that the rift between the two African tectonic plates caused a vast mountain range to rise, segmenting the heavily treed rainforest that spanned the continent west to east. Rainclouds coming on westerly winds would rise up the western slopes of the range and dump all their moisture, leaving East Africa to dry out and begin the gradual transition from rainforest to savannah. Forced slowly from the trees to the savannah, the theory goes, our pre-human ancestors needed to see over the high grasses, so they stood, which freed their hands for hand signal communication and eventually speech ("watch out! Here comes the lion in the tall grass!"). Watching the raging fire propel Mary's essence into the sky, I reflected "how wonderful that her ashes will be forever in the place where we humans first became human?"

Soon the heat became so intense we needed to leave the raised platform. The businessmen placed Wade and the four of us on the lawn surrounding the pyre, closest to the fire. Everyone else stood respectfully behind the five survivors. One by one we approached the magnificent conflagration, offered our prayer or message, and sat back down together. Realizing Mary's cells were now flowing into the air, released from her earthly body, I found myself breathing deeply, trying to capture what little bits of my beloved Mary I could, drawing them into my lungs and maybe somehow merging them into my own cells. It felt calming and good. "She's in my heart forever already," I figured, "let me get as much of her into the rest of my body as I can." Feeling clever, I tapped Trevor on the shoulder to share my brilliant idea. The Biology major smiled and said 'Dad, we already have 50% of mom in our D.N.A. We're good." I laughed out loud, tears filling my eyes again.

"Of course, of course!," I chuckled, "you lucky buggers." I believe they are comforted in a strange way by that thought. I know I am. Mary lives on in the bodies of these three wonderful people, Trevor, Becky, and John. "I will nurture her soul in these three for the rest of my life, I swear," I vowed.

As darkness fell on the little sanctuary compound, we were mesmerized by the eternal inferno in our midst. Outside the walls, other frightening screeching and wailing began. It sounded like a furious religious leader exhorting his flock to jihad. The fire would burn all night, reaching 1000 degrees Fahrenheit they told us, and the businessmen were anxious to go home to their families for dinner. We all piled back into our bus, feeling inexplicably changed. A voice in the semi-dark bus remarked "I feel much lighter, pleasantly relieved somehow." I noticed a true peace in Trevor's eyes. John, Becky, and I were quiet, reflective and calmed. "This ceremony was perfect," we all agreed. The African Environments people arranged a warm, welcoming dinner for Wade and us, which felt like a family gathering. WE all chatted warmly, like long lost friends, feeling lighter. When we finally arrived at Cabins 3 and 4 after dinner we were exhausted, relaxed, peaceful and spiritually full. We were able to sleep a little better, knowing Mary was on her way and we would be going home tomorrow. The sniffling slowly abated. We slept.

Next morning I looked at myself in the mirror and noticed the deep indentations in my abdomen. I smiled, realizing Mary would have been happy as she began her journey last night. It wouldn't have been because I lost 10 pounds on the mountain, but because she did, as well. Through our 30 years together Mary was hyper-vigilant about her weight. Five pounds too much and she felt "fat" and grumpy. Five pounds less than average and she felt "hot and sexy." I honestly could barely tell the difference. I adored her at all of her weights. But, I knew that morning in Tanzania, Mary went off on her next journey looking thin and feeling "gorgeous." You go, girl.

Saturday, January 7th 2006. In the bright sunshine that morning in Arusha, the Hindu compound seemed like a totally different place: no flaming violence, no screeching, no wrenching emotional trauma, just quiet and light. The ash pit was rendered down to white and gray dust, sprinkled with bright white pieces of vertebrae. "Those must be some tough bones to withstand 1000 degrees overnight," someone remarked. According to Hindu custom, the remains must find water. "They will make it to one of the sacred lakes nearby. The ashes will go to the river close to here," one of the businessmen informed us.

The priest commenced the final chapter of the ceremony for Mary and Betty. He had us remove our shoes and place flowers, beads and fragrances into beautifully carved rosewood boxes, which Richard somehow found on very short notice. The boxes already contained their ashes. We adorned the outside of the pit with flowers and incense at the corners. We threw flowers into the pit as well. Next, the priest instructed Trevor, the oldest son, and Wade, the husband, in placing their respective boxes near their hearts, mouths, heads and shoulders as he chanted. We walked around the pit barefoot and placed more flowers. He took our hands in his and, in broken English, advised us how to proceed after this tragedy. "Young men react to death by fighting, young ladies by worrying." We may have missed the more important lessons, lost in translation, but we left the Hindu sanctuary compound in the middle of Arusha, Tanzania very relieved and at peace.

As I stood in line at Kilimanjaro International Airport, goodbyes all said, tears shed, grasping the rosewood box holding Mary's ashes, I was overcome by a wave of emotions. I was awed by the majesty and rightness of the way Mary's life ended and her next journey began, in a burst of energy and light and heat. I felt a deep gratitude to the people who took care of us these last few days, making myriad decisions large and small, all designed to ease our journey. "The universe is a warm, welcoming place," I felt, "at least most of the time." Then the thought struck me that Mary and I almost lost our marriage partnership eleven years earlier. Had it not been for her fortitude and courage, our storybook romance would have been nipped in the bud, ripped out by the roots, just as so many other marriages seemed to die all around us....

Chapter 7. "Burning Down and Rebuilding"

By the late eighties our marriage was outwardly successful, as lush and green as the rainforest at the foot of Mount Kilimanjaro, but inside it was as barren and lifeless as the moonscape atop Big Mama. Mary and I were able to put on a happy face in public, but the weight of our housing choices, lifestyle decisions, family history and business pressure was ready to crush our marriage. At home we barely spoke except to carp at each other, and we both felt despondent, hopeless and angry. The kids felt it. They always do. Something had to give.

Having made a profit on three successive house sale/purchase transactions, and feeling like we were "can't lose" real estate geniuses (giving no credit to the housing bubble of the 80's), we stretched ourselves thin to squeak into what was my dream house - the twin sister to the "Home Alone" house. With its circular drive, 7 bedrooms, 800 feet of hedges, sculpted round shrubs, it was a "wow" house, and considerably more than we could afford. When I requested a quote from a landscaper to maintain the property for a year, the reply was $17,000. I was seriously unprepared for that budget bomb. My dad purchased a riding mower for us as a housewarming gift, and I spent four hours a weekend on lawn and bush upkeep. The two yellow lab puppies we got, brother and sister, dug our backyard into a minefield. When I awoke one morning to see crows ripping up the few spots the dogs hadn't excavated from my dead lawn in order to eat the juicy grubs below, I wanted to scream and cry uncle. Visions of $50,000 re-sod jobs danced in my head. It was way too much house, and I possessed not nearly enough patience.

For Mary's part, she managed to overwhelm herself with child raising frenzy, overseeing the constant repair work by contractors in the house, handling car accident and malfunction issues, and worrying about her struggling California family. Running from soccer game to baseball practice to swimming, play dates and parties non-stop, Mary at one point became convinced she had come down with shoulder cancer. One Saturday I noticed her reaching far across our no-frills Plymouth Voyager minivan from the front seat, grimacing as she strained to unlock the manual sliding back door. She was relieved by my diagnosis: "you don't have cancer, but you might ask the kids to open that door from now on." Money was short, but emergencies and urgent house repairs were in bountiful supply. I didn't seem to be around enough when she needed me. My business so drained me that when she asked me to read the kids stories at bedtime, sometimes I just couldn't muster the energy. She got so angry. I couldn't understand. Our physical closeness evaporated. Maybe to vent her anger at me, she would sometimes flirt extravagantly with other husbands at dinner parties. I couldn't understand this behavior either. "Oh, stop," she would say the next morning, "it was the wine. I was only kidding."

My business was under severe pressure as well, mostly from poor decisions by my partner, my father. The real estate bubble in the late 80's burst inexorably, and he refused to react in a timely manner. In a desperate attempt to rescue his real estate company, he confiscated all the emergency cash from the stronger sister company, the insurance agency, which I was responsible for. For months we could barely make payroll. He put our business in serious jeopardy. I was furious and scared all at the same time. All my personal cash and borrowing capacity was tied up in my massive new trophy house, so I was powerless to help. My stress level was off the charts.

One night in the kitchen it all came to a head. I was washing dishes after dinner and listening to a typical diatribe about what a poor excuse I was for a father, husband and partner. Something in me snapped. "Let me ask you a question, Mary," I started, "why don't you just go to California for a while, if you're so miserable? We'll be OK. If you decide to stay out there, I'll post the following job description: 'woman needed to help raise 3 healthy children in 7 bedroom suburban mansion, cleaning person and au pair provided, nice cars available, all expenses paid, occasional sex with decent husband requested.' How long will the sign up line for that job be? If you think this job is so horrible, QUIT. Do us both a favor!" Looking back, it seems cruel, but we simply couldn't continue the way were going. The once euphoric romance now seemed like an overgrown tinderbox forest just waiting for a match.

The details of the unfortunate indiscretion that followed are immaterial here. It wasn't entered into easily or quickly or without massive hesitation. When it was eventually confessed, the anger on Mary's part now took on a laser-like focus. I left the "Home Alone" house for a few weeks to live at a friend's empty apartment. The first weekend Mary took the kids to a relative's house, but other than that I saw them every single day. I knew I couldn't live without seeing them every day. At my father's suggestion I spent three days alone in Key West to straighten my head out. I came back and told Mary I wanted to move back into the house. I offered to stay in the pool house, but she suggested the guest bedroom, next to the Master bedroom where she was. I would have slept in the boiler room or in the bath tub if it meant being under my kids' roof every day.

The expected thing to do in this circumstance is to call lawyers and begin divorce proceedings. Certainly there was a cacophony of advice from angry, but well-meaning friends of Mary to "kick the bum out. Leave him. All men are no good." I certainly didn't want that, and Mary agreed to see a marriage mediator with me. At the big conference table in the mediator's office, the lawyer surgically sketched out how our assets would be divided and our options for child visitation. Mary and I looked at each other, our chairs pushed back simultaneously, and we said "we need a minute." Sitting in the car down in the parking lot, we cried, gulping for air, terrified at the prospect of watching our marriage dissolve. "I don't want this," one of us said. "Neither do I." "Will you go to counseling with me?," Mary asked. "I will do anything it takes," I said. "It won't be easy," she warned. "I know. I'm ready," I agreed.

And so were planted the first seeds in the re-growing of our burned down forest marriage. I give Mary all the credit. She could easily have given in to the chorus of angry voices. It would have felt good to exact retribution. Mary certainly had many opportunities to vent her vitriol about me to the children. She never once did, although I bet she bit through her tongue a few times. Through the months that followed Mary was the heroine. She had the fortitude and bravery and courage to keep planting seeds, re-growing the forest, allowing a wonderful second marriage to take root amid the ruins of the first, and flourish.

Mary began her own journey of self-discovery and rebirth alongside me in counseling. Guided imagery brought her a vision of "little Mary" tugging on her mom's apron at the kitchen sink in their San Mateo home, needing some attention. In the image, Mom never turned to comfort little Mary. She took that hard. Our drill sergeant marriage counselor proceeded to strip away all of our defenses. Mary once said, in the early going, "this isn't the life I would have chosen." The wise doctor stopped her right in her tracks. "Did you hear what you just said?" He continued, "Exactly who did choose your life for you? Your mom? Your dad? Your sisters? Your friends?" At each question he paused and she said "no". At "Did Scott choose your life for you?," she hesitated and finally realized "no." When we both fully accepted responsibility for our breakup, more seeds got planted, more sunshine poured in. It was elicited that whenever papa Harvey read books to little Mary she felt loved and listened to. Whenever I later refused to read bedtime stories to my kids, my refusal hurt Mary terribly. It was as if her dad had rejected her in her childhood days. When I realized this connection, a light went off in my head, a mystery was solved, and I cried and cried. I promised to read to the kids and to Mary every night. I never knew. More seeds planted, more rain, more sunshine.

It wasn't easy. We fought and cried, and struggled to understand each other. The process took months and years. At a remote beach in Puerto Rico we threw our first marriage wedding rings into the ocean. We had new ones made the next week. Our second marriage had begun, the seedlings were now saplings. We were wiser, stronger and better. We almost lost each other once, so we fully realized how fragile and precious this second chance was.

As thrilled as Mary and the kids and I were that we averted disaster and reknitted our broken marriage, our extended families were equally excited. It was to these two groups, in California and on the East Coast, that we turned, as we got off the KLM airplane from Amsterdam to New York that January 8th of 2006. One question I needed to work out, as I clutched the rosewood box carrying Mary's ashes to my chest, was where to spread them?

Chapter 8. "Remembering Mary"

By the time we walked into JFK International Airport arrivals the four of us were all cried out, resigned to attempt the impossible, carrying on without Mary. We had been warned to expect the media, but they didn't show up in earnest until the next day, Monday. My sisters Jane Stuart and Sue Patrolia had flown to Amsterdam to surprise us and shepherd us home. Two more caring sisters you will never find. Our house was buzzing with organizers, principally Mickey Clement, Mary's best friend, her hiking buddies Mary Ann Pettit, Beth Dannhauser, and Ruthann Markowitz, and my sisters. Trevor and John had girlfriends and pals around. Becky was surrounded by girlfriends. The company was distracting and energetic. Becky asked her friends to go home at night. I went to bed at 9:00pm every night and awoke at 5:30am to write. I needed to try to make sense of what had happened to us. The well-wishers started streaming in Monday morning, and the stream rose to a flood tide by Wednesday. Newsday put our picture on its front cover, the one of us all smiling in front of the backlit, beautiful Big Mama. Daily News carried their interview with me, ABC lead off their 6:00pm newscast with our story, CBS featured it as well, but FOX was too late to get the story to run with it. With the media flurry completed and the flow of friends and associates ebbing, it was time to focus on the memorials: January 12th in Huntington, New York and January 15th in Amador, California.

"Where should we hold Mary's Memorial?" asked the Huntington group. "How about the Old First Church?" someone suggested. Since my family had been members of the church for generations, I knew well the historic fellowship room could handle 200-300 people. Something told me that might be too small, so I suggested Coindre Hall, a huge sprawling Gold Coast mansion now owned by Suffolk County. When the $12,000 estimate came back, I gasped. Marge quickly volunteered to fund one half of the bill, then Quentin offered to pay the entire tab. I was touched and grateful. Mary's desires for her funeral were always clear to me. I could hear her words in my ear, "cremation, no burial. Motown music, nothing depressing. No black clothes. I want a party with noise and laughter. And, if you mess this up, I will haunt you forever," she would laugh. I hand selected the Motown playlist, Mickey found Lessings to cater the event, nephew James Stuart prepared a slide show of the cremation event, and I wrote my eulogy, covered in tears.

We drove up to Coindre Hall the night of the 12th in the dark. There was a quiet reverence and an air of expectation in our pickup truck. The hulking Gold Coast mansion was lit up, splendid in its former glory. Holy cow, there were a million cars! Entering the grandiose lobby, I was mobbed. So many familiar faces lifted my spirits. Marge ushered me past the surprising throng, and the Lessings Event Manager parked me in the huge ballroom in the back. He patrolled the greeting line, which at one point grew to 90 minutes long. I hugged everybody, whether I recognized them or not. I was teary and giddy all at the same time. "All this for little, unpretentious, limelight-avoiding, San Mateo girl Mary Lou Salzman Sammis," I wrote later. Foolishly, I felt briefly like a rock star, with fans lining up for a chance to hug me. Looking back, Marge was a very effective drill sergeant, moving me along, keeping me from talking all night long. Without her, we might still be there. Estimates were that 600-800 people attended that night, many more than some Congressmen or Senators draw, according to the Lessings Manager. Wow.

7:30 came and the shepherds gathered the multitude into the cavernous ballroom, the Motown music was muted, and a hush fell: it was tribute time. Mickey Clement and Sue Sherman, Mary's oldest and dearest friends gave sweet, nervous, warm remembrances of Mary amid sniffles and laughs. 20 year old John bravely offered his adoring tribute to his mom, finishing with the Hunter S. Thompson quote: "Life should not be a journey to the grave with the intention of arriving safely in a pretty and well preserved body, but rather to skid in broadside in a cloud of smoke, thoroughly used up, totally worn out, and loudly proclaiming 'Wow! What a Ride!'" His mom Mary died with her boots on, living her dream. John is my hero for standing up like that for his mom. My hat is off to him.

When I rose to speak I felt the world stop. I gripped the mike and knew in my heart I was ready to pour out my soul. I paused to look out over the hundreds and hundreds of souls and felt infused with energy. Mary would steady my heart and clear my voice, I knew. She knew I needed to touch these grieving hearts and give them her peace. Thanking the travelers for coming from far and wide, I talked about Mary's love for me and the kids, which extended to them as well. Looking into their moist, glistening eyes I told them two stories bookending my 30 year journey with Mary: the First Date/Half Moon Bay/Mateus/Volkswagen story, which brought down the house in gales of laughter; and the brave story of Mary's last few hours, how she wouldn't give up, even suffering from depletion and exhaustion. Their sniffles and tears choked me up.

To finish I gave them Mary's last message to us in the lonely hotel in Arusha, Tanzania, and I could feel a vast welling up of grief and fears and angst, and a powerful gladness everyone felt for having the privilege of knowing wonderful Mary Lou. My voice cracked badly at the end. The emotion was crystal clear, the message strong: "Don't wait. Get to work NOW on moving toward the life you imagined. I didn't wait and you must not either. I love you." The crowd gasped. I never felt anything remotely like it in my life. Mary's story had brought them right into my heart so they could see her one more time. Wow.

When I signed off there was an enormous ovation, an outpouring for Mary and her family, and I hugged the kids and Mickey and Sue. The last hour of the celebration was a blur, but I think I hugged every single one of the multitude while the Motown music serenaded us. Giddy from exhaustion, they hustled me and the kids out to the red pickup truck and we drove home, exulting. Even though the house was full and pulsing with energy and love, I collapsed, a zombie, at 10:30. The limo arrived the next morning to whisk us off to California at 6:15am.

Mary's big, bustling, bumptious, beautiful, beloved family was gathered together in Amador, California at her sister Amy's house. A sprawling farm ranch house on 80 acres an hour southeast of Sacramento, Amy's house has been the family gathering place since their mom, also named Amy, passed away. The four sisters knew "someone had to be the mom," and Amy was elected by acclamation. January 14th was gray, glowering and miserable. By ten we had eaten some breakfast, but it was clear Becky was hurting. "Wanna take a walk?" I offered. She sniffled "yes." Shuffling down the long, curving driveway, Becky choked "she won't be there for my wedding, or for the birth of my kids." I felt we were both falling, tumbling down into a bottomless black abyss. I held her, and we both dissolved. Parents always try to take away their kids' pain. This pain was excruciatingly horrible and I felt powerless to mitigate it in any way. We rocked slowly for a while. Then I whispered "sweetie, don't look up the mountain ahead at the impossible trail. It's too scary, too huge. Look at the next one step, stop to breathe, and then take the next step. The future will take care of itself. As far as the wedding and your babies, you will have to make do with me. They say I have a feminine side, maybe a little rusty, but try me, OK? I WILL BE THERE, I promise. And so will mom and her sisters and my sisters." She cried some more and then managed a smile. We walked some more in silence, and the sadness passed. I knew it would return, however, many times.

Sister Shirley assembled 25 or 30 of us in a handholding circle in Amy's big cozy living room. Mostly family, with a few friends sprinkled in, all a trifle embarrassed. Shirley started the story-telling, followed by Amy, both bringing some warm laughter. Then Joan Johnson, Mary's closest work friend at Industrial Indemnity, took her turn. Joan was one of my suspects in the ticket/note mystery, so when she began to tell "a story about how Mary and Scott met in San Francisco," my ears perked up. "I knew Mary was very interested in this cute new Safety Engineer down on the fourth floor," she started off, "so she buys these tickets to a jazz concert...." There was an explosion in my head. WHAAAAT? The mystery was solved! Mary bought the tickets?!!! I made a huge scene, gesticulating in mock outrage that Mary had hoodwinked me all these years into believing she knew nothing about the tickets. How many opportunities did she have in our 30 years to reveal that little secret? The formerly somber group was bent over double at my shock and consternation. Having grabbed the spotlight, I decided to tell the cremation/deep breathing story and Trevor's reassuring me. That elicited happiness too. I finished with Mary's revelation message and choked up, unable to continue. Everyone dissolved. Such sweet, honest emotions for a wonderful, unpretentious San Mateo girl.

Back in the hotel in Amador, and in my own quiet room in Huntington, I would go to bed early and wake up in the dark, lowering my heart rate, opening myself up to a contact with Mary, an image, a whisper. I wrote in my journal early the following Saturday morning in Huntington "I am still in a dream state. Most of me accepts what has happened, part refuses. I keep expecting the creaky automatic garage door to squeak open, the grocery bags to bustle in the hallway, and Mary's sweet voice to cry out 'Hi, guys!' What I wouldn't give to have her back." That morning I cleared out her duffel bag from Kilimanjaro and found a hair scrunchie – I nearly lost it. The little things. I can't bear giving away her clothes and hairdryer and personal stuff. I want to turn her study into a shrine that I can sit in and feel her presence. I want to fill the house with pictures of her.

It's comforting to believe Mary's with her dad Harvey, her mom Amy, and my mom Ellie. People like her friend Didi Finlayson say they feel Mary all the time. I don't, sadly. I wait for her in those quiet, dark moments in our bed. I am open to a message. I feel she would say "I'm fine. I love you with all my heart. I'm sorry to be gone, but I'm happy. Please fill the kids with love as much as you can, and be happy. I'm waiting." Such a good heart. Mary tried so hard her whole life to be a good person. Yet she was SO hard on herself, listening always to the negative messages in her head. Way too hard on herself. If she had only loved herself HALF as much as I did.....

"The kids are struggling, Mare, you know," I told her, in my journal, the night after we four visited Bill and Lucy in New Jersey. At their lovely home, I had gotten drawn into a blow-by-blow post-mortem of the events of the day she died on the mountain. "I got chills, but I benefited from the discussion," I explained to Mary. "The kids later said it felt like someone was standing on their chests for several hours. I didn't realize how bad it was for them. They just don't want to go through the nightmare anymore. They lost their mom. Even worse, you were the best mom anyone ever had, by acclamation of their friends, ALL of them. It's an unthinkable loss for Trevor, Beck and John. They will be struggling for YEARS. Please help them if you can," I begged her. "Quiet their fears, fill their hearts with your smile. Let them know you are with them. Harve came to you when you needed him in Cabo. Please go to them. They need you now."

The children and I were deep in a morass of sorrow. We needed to work our way back to the lighter, happier world we had inhabited before that day on Mount Kilimanjaro. I'd seen Mary struggle after our first marriage burned down. She fought and clawed and learned and made herself into a stronger person, and gave our second marriage a chance to flourish. In the midst of the darkness of her passing, I needed to draw strength from her rebirth from her own dark days.....

Chapter 9. "Mary Flourishes"

Mary blossomed in the days and years after our near breakup. She opened herself to new ways of thinking, forced herself to explore, looked into herself, and learned volumes. She flourished. She lead by example. I believe she may have lived under one cloud of fear, at least, during our "first marriage:" the worry was "how would I survive if Scott were to leave me?" After successfully making it through my brief absence, she realized "I can do this. I can make it on my own." Occasionally she would remind me "By the way, sucker, if you ever pull this stunt again, I am gone and I'm not looking back." I got the message. It worked for me.

One of Mary's first restorative journeys was Outward Bound. O.B. describes its purpose this way: "to impel its participants into values-forming experiences." Using a combination of intense togetherness/group projects and utter aloneness, vigorous, exhausting treks and fear-provoking challenges, Outward Bound pushes its graduates well beyond their self-imposed limitations. Just when you think you can't push another step or stroke, O.B. forces you to find the inner reserves to push another hour or three. Mary's chosen adventure/ordeal was to spend two weeks on the desert beaches of Cabo San Lucas on the Baja Peninsula, sea kayaking and hiking all day, eating and living without plumbing or showers, and sleeping on the beach. Two days in she was convinced she didn't have the strength and tearfully asked to resign. The guides talked her out of it. Soon she toughened up, got a little mad, and found her way. Dropped off far away on a deserted beach for her two day "solo" with only basic food and water, a plastic tarp and nylon cord, Mary felt the panic rise again. "How will I avoid total dehydration without a tent? I can't figure out how to tie this tarp up!" she cried in the desert. Suddenly her mind quieted, and she heard her father Harvey's voice say "Sis, find some small rocks, wrap one in each corner of your tarp, and tie the cord around the bundled rocks. You'll see it works. Try it." Mary sobbed with joy, grateful to get the advice, and so heartwarmed to know her dad was watching out for her.

One summer not long after Outward Bound, Mary undertook a grueling and emotionally charged physical challenge, climbing the 5,000 foot tall Half Dome in Yosemite National Park, California with her 20-something nephews. After five hours hiking uphill to reach the base of Half Dome, she began the treacherous climb up the bald rock spine of the mountain. The gradient feels like 90% or straight up when you climb it, but it's probably only 60-70%, still extremely daunting. The boys had gone on ahead, so Mary sweated this part on her own. Hand over hand on the iron rails, pulling herself up the steep granite face, she was exhausted and sobbing by the time she reached the flat top. Looking out over the sheer one mile deep drop straight down to the valley,

Mary realized she wanted to have her ashes spilled over this magnificent place after she died and was cremated. There was a stiff breeze coming up the cliff of Half Dome that day. She mentioned to me later that I would need to check the wind direction on top of Half Dome before I threw her ashes over the cliff, otherwise I would get a face full. "Sure, sure, honey," I said, never thinking it would happen.

Our marriage counselors provided more insights. One noticed Mary's obsession with managing her kids' every emotional crisis. "By protecting your children every moment, you not only preclude them from developing self reliance," the advisor said, "but you rob yourself of time for you to reflect and develop your own talent and strengths. You must let go some and regain your balance." Mary took that advice to heart. It was in conflict with her selfless upbringing, but she learned to "Do for Mary first, then help others." The next time the airline flight attendant intoned "Place you own oxygen mask on first, then adjust the masks of those around you," she got the larger message.

We both struggled to understand why our "first marriage" burned down, and eventually lessons emerged. While I did have some anger and resentment, what I did was out of selfishness, fear and poor judgment. Mary was very hurt, but much of what occurred had nothing really to do with her, but mostly with my own shortcomings. Slowly it dawned on her, also with the help of counseling, that "it's not always about me." People are seldom out to hurt us intentionally – they act out their own needs - but we happen to catch the shrapnel, to become collateral damage. A spiritual advisor convinced Mary that "Scott was asleep, programmed to act the way he did. Now he is awake." Mary viewed this as an explanation, not an excuse, and gained a measure of clarity and understanding.

Mary painstakingly earned a Masters Degree in English as a Second Language at CW Post College on Long Island. To return to college in her late forties and remaster algebra and trigonometry, among other subjects, was a frightening, daunting experience. Becky and I were patient tutors, she struggled, and finally got it. What a joy to see her face light up as problem after problem fell before her new found analytic tools. I flew her mom Amy out from California for the proud graduation day. Mary was beaming. She also learned in time she could sell Real Estate with a partner, fix leaky pipes around our house, and be instrumental in raising several Habitat for Humanity houses. She was becoming a true Renaissance woman.

Mom Amy's battle with Alzheimer's disease both stoked Mary's own health fears and further fueled her determination to "get on with the adventure." Watching the slow, relentless deterioration of her mom, and being with her as she succumbed, seared Mary forever. "Never let an adventure pass you by," she would tell all of us. In short order we traveled to China, the Galapagos Islands, Australia, New

Zealand, Costa Rica, and Zimbabwe, Africa. She inspired the children to travel by themselves to Costa Rica, Europe and Ecuador. Her last trip before Kilimanjaro was a solo journey to Oaxaca, Mexico. For five weeks she explored the spiritual world of these gentle people and encouraged her own spirit to

TL - (B) Amy, Mary, Shirley, Amy, (F) Trevor, Ashley, Andrew; TM - Mary; TR - (B) Gary, Amy, (F) Sally, Shirley, Mary, Amy, Steve
BL - People going up cables on Half Dome; BM - Mary, Amy; BR - Mary

blossom.

Our "second marriage" was not without its hard times and dark moments; we needed to stay vigilant and nurture the new growth forest. Each of the three children bumped up against the disciplinary limits of High School. John was the champion in that area. We were in contact with the school's Chief Disciplinary Officer, Mr. Noce, so frequently that we each had instant voice recognition. As Mary moved toward the finish line of graduating the last child through High School, she became more frustrated and less tolerant. She couldn't wait to remove herself from the day-to-day child management functions and enter the new territory of "it's my time." Mary wanted to be out exploring New York City, hiking, and traveling. I simultaneously became more of a homebody. She worried more when the kids were in the house. I worried more when they were outside the house. When the daily battle to get John out of bed and into class was finally finished, Mary was ecstatic!

We tussled over finances and retirement, and rehashed the indiscretion, always with honesty and passion, but careful not to lay any new bricks on the resentment wall. Mary's philosophy became "live for today, for tomorrow may never come." I was more inclined to save and prepare for the future. She would say "let's chuck the expensive lifestyle and move to a cabin in a warmer climate." I wasn't ready. I would say "Be patient, our ship will come in one day and we'll have plenty of money." She'd screw up her pretty face and say "I want to see the money now. Put it right here, in my palm, so I can see it." Mostly able to forgive and forget, my sweet Mary Lou would sometimes have a bad day and feel the need to berate me one more time over my past mistakes. I figured I deserved it. There's a concept called "the trust bank" in which partners make deposits by fulfilling promises, showing up on time, etc. and withdrawals by lying, cheating, being late, and so forth. I was busy rebuilding the trust account we had badly depleted, so while the rebukes hurt, I knew the balances in the trust bank were growing, day by day.

TL - Shirley, Mary, Amy; TM - Shirl, Steve, Amy, Amy, Gary, Mary, Sally; TR - Steve, Sally, Mary, Amy, Shirley, Gary
BL - Mary; BM - Mary with family on China trip; BR - Mary, Amy

The children watched the development of our "second marriage" with rapt attention. Of course they knew there was trouble well before the breakup, suffered during my absence, and rejoiced when we both fully committed ourselves to building a stronger partnership the second time around. They drew inspiration from Mary's bravery and grace. They watched as she pushed herself in new directions. They felt her relentless urging to "take the chance, try the new thing, never let an adventure pass you by." They each screwed up their courage and traveled on their own, without us, and were each profoundly affected by their individual Outward Bound experiences. As much as they were over-managed as youngsters, they grew into strong, self-reliant, independent thinkers with what Trevor calls fully functioning "bullshit detectors." And, when the major tragedy of their young lives occurred in 2006, they turned to each other, and to traveling, for strength......

Chapter 10. "Europe and My Old Friend the Blues"

Before Kilimanjaro Becky and Trevor had planned to spend a month or so in Thailand, Cambodia and Vietnam, countries they had never visited, directly after our Africa adventure. The crushing events on the mountain, coupled with the emergence of the Avian Flu epidemic in the Far East, prompted me to scuttle those plans. I imagined the two of them in the Cambodian countryside just as the Avian Flu outbreak forced the closure of the borders, preventing them from exiting and me from getting to them. That thought was too horrible to accept. I suggested they spend two months in Europe where I could at least extract them in an emergency. The outpouring of grief in our little town and the rawness of the loss of Mary I knew would subject the kids to daily doses of "I'm so sorry for your loss" from crying friends if they stayed at home. Better, I thought, to distract them with backpacking and museums in the Old Country. I guess I really didn't believe they would stop crying.

And they didn't. John had bravely stated, right after the California Memorial, that he needed to get back to Santa Barbara City College to redouble his efforts to become a doctor. He stood tall on the mountain in the crisis and stayed so clear-headed when chaos reigned and death lurked. I think he felt the need to "charge" his studies. "No time to grieve," he thought, "Mom would want me to get on with my dream." Putting him on that westbound plane broke my heart, however. For two weeks he soldiered on. Then he broke down, unable to focus or study or even give a damn. He could only cry. John was fearful that if he screwed up the current semester he would blow his entire medical career dream. I tried to reassure him his meltdown was "completely natural, even expected and predictable. With a huge intellectual challenge ahead of you and no emotional support in Santa Barbara, how could this not happen?" I recommended he postpone the school work for a semester and consider joining his siblings in Europe. John was leaning, but unconvinced, when Becky took the phone from me. "Listen, John," she said in her beautiful and understatedly profound way, "none of us knows how to do this." The wisdom that issues from this quiet one never ceases to amaze me. I could almost feel the relief in John 3,000 miles away. The next day he decided to come home and join the Europe journey.

I hugged the kids in the dark on the morning of February 9th 2006. We were all leaving on jet planes, me to Florida to visit my father for a few days and Trevor, Becky and John to tour Europe. I begged them to take care of each other and come back safe. I didn't want the hugs to end, I loved them so desperately. I didn't know what I would do the next 60 days without them. If I really wanted to send myself into a tailspin,

I would let my mind consider when they all scatter to Santa Barbara and Washington, DC after Europe and leave me here alone with the dog, but without Mary. I couldn't let myself go down that road, on purpose.

I didn't hear from the kids until four days after they left and Becky called from Barcelona, distraught and crying. "The abyss grabs me every night, dad, and I cry until I fall asleep. I don't think I can continue." They had met their uncle Jeff Murphy in a hotel in Barcelona - he was there on business - and he greeted them with condolences. They lost it completely. Familiar faces, warm wishes, and "look out, here comes the abyss." I offered the option of coming home, but Becky said forlornly "it would be worse at home." I urged her to keep calling me anytime of the day or night, ask for hugs from her brothers, and try walking until the tears stop. She sniffled and agreed. "Goodbye Dad, I love you." That killed me.

John called the next day, the same way, dissolved in tears. I gave the same advice and told him "I think about you every minute of every day." "Same, same Dad. I love you." I ached to be there with them and hug them all up. Trevor seemed to be holding up better. He had his girlfriend Sarah with him to comfort him, and he was practicing his Zen. "I feel the emotional wave coming," he explained, "I recognize and label the feeling, I step back in my mind, acknowledging it, and soon it passes through me. It is only an emotion. I am me."

I felt the abyss yawn for me frequently during the weeks

in February, the darkness calling. Just telling the story of the mountain or even seeing someone who hasn't heard, choked me up. I tried keeping myself busy with tying up Mary's loose ends, filing the travel insurance death claim, business travails including an employee lawsuit over a termination, dinners with friends, YMCA affairs, returning to my personal trainer, etc. The quiet times alone, either in bed or driving, were when the moroseness would set in. In the pickup truck one night I heard Lee Ann Rimes sing "If you have the chance to sit it out or dance, I hope you dance." Mary always wanted to dance I remember, and the tears flowed. The next morning I awoke on the wrong side of the bed and decided to throw away all of Mary's personal hygiene products, hair stuff, soaps, skin creams, etc. I couldn't begin to imagine giving away or discarding her clothes yet - way too hard. But I was a little angry and the lotions bags filled up and wound up in the big garbage cans in the garage. I felt sad all day, wondering how even parting with Mary's meaningless stuff could depress me so strongly.

In Nashville at the Grand Ol' Opry, years earlier, Mary and I discovered T. Graham Brown and his earthy, heart-rending story songs. In my favorite "My Old Friend the Blues" he sings:

> *Just when every ray of hope was gone,*
> *I should have known that you would come along.*
> *I can't believe I ever doubted you,*

My old friend the Blues
Another lonely night in a nameless town,
If sleep don't take me first, you'll come around,
'Cause I know I can always count on you,
My old friend the Blues.

With Brown's help I learned to manage my sadness. Rather than push off the blackness when it tapped me on the shoulder, I decided to stop and embrace it fully. If possible I would play some music and bring it on, tears and all. Strangely, I came to a point where I almost welcomed the tap on the shoulder from my old friend. I let it rip through me and pass on. It its wake was always peace, and sometimes even a quiet euphoria.

Graham Brown's songs about battles with alcoholism, child molestation and Alzheimer's are killers, but when I walked the dog at sunset on deserted Asharoken beach at sunset one day, what knocked me on my ass was "As If You Didn't Know." It goes like this:

Every time we're alone like this, there's so much I want to say.
We both know what we're feeling, but words just get in the way.
But tonight, I want to hold you, and tell you I still love you so.
It feels so good to say the words again, as if you didn't know.

You were there to reach out and rescue me,
When I was sinking helplessly and nobody else believed.
You were there to help me rise above,
With your warm and tender love, you never once gave up.
I love you so. As if you didn't know.

I know I told Mary a million times how much I owed her for having the courage to save our marriage. I know she felt like a wimp who "gave in and took him back," but I knew otherwise. The easy thing would have been to poison the kids against me and give in to the angry shrill voices urging her to "screw him, the bastard, just leave him." She took the hard way out, the courageous way. She truly rescued me and our marriage. I could only hope she died knowing how much I loved her and how much I owed her...

John, Becky, Trevor and I were reunited in Florence, Italy during the second week of March, 2006, halfway through their 60 day sojourn. When I first caught sight of them in the Florence airport I jumped up and down like a kid at Christmas or Niko the dog when she's offered a walk around the block. I cried big tears of joy, so, so happy. The week flew by. Such a magnificent, uplifting city full of history, art, discovery, and promise. My kids were happy to see me too, but I could see they were shell-shocked still. They didn't seem to care where they went next and would gladly take direction and suggestions from the two others in their group. They were also worried about re-entry into their real lives, I could tell. I knew Becky was particularly worried about living in DC with Trevor, as planned, and leaving me to fend for myself. Believe me, so was I.

The week was warm and wonderful, even if the temperature was chilly. We had many chances to talk one on one and just be together. Our happiest family times were always traveling, exploring, discovering. We felt Mary/Mom around us all the time, beaming. The last night I was with them in Florence, predictably, was awful. Outside the Internet café where the boys were retrieving emails and planning next stops, Becky withdrew to quietly meltdown. I followed her out to find her swallowed by the abyss. "When I'm in this black hole, Dad," she sniffled, "I can't imagine a life I want to live." I wrapped her in my arms and got her to walk with me. Soon the mood lightened. We met Mary's sister Shirley, who was every bit as destroyed as we are at Mary's passing, and the girls hugged and cried again. The separation scene at the Firenze Train Station had a Bogart/<u>Casablanca</u> feel to it, without the rain. Becky and John were sobbing, I was crying, Trevor was misting, trying to tough it out. I boarded the train finally, but came out again to hug them all one more time and tell them I loved them.

After Italy and Greece, the children returned to Spain, and the calls started again. The sights and sounds of a March fireworks display in Valencia, Spain brought back the bombardment on Kilimanjaro, and Becky "freaked out" again. Two days later she was dissolved again, wanting to come home. She was so concerned about her future, what to do next, and was so lost. "I think I might need to stay with you for awhile, Dad," she said, "you need some care too." My heart soared hearing that. I counseled patience and reminded her of her words to John: "none of us knows how to do this." I could feel her smile on the phone. The boys were distracted by flirtatious females in Spain, but I implored them to be attentive to their quiet sister. "She is the most important person on the planet to you now, Please pay attention." They got the message.

One afternoon as the sun was setting back in New York, I was feeling morose and idly checked my cell phone messages: zero. Without thinking I scrolled down the list of saved numbers and stopped at Mary's cell #. Gulp. I called it and her sweet, upbeat voice answered asking me to leave a message. "I love you," I gushed, "and I miss you. This is too hard for me to handle alone. The kids will be home soon and off on their own paths. The nest will be empty. You are supposed to be here with me. It's not fair. How could you do this?" Clicking the END button, I was consumed with guilt about blaming Mary for what happened on Kilimanjaro. She certainly did not choose to be killed by a freak rock slide and abandon us in the peak of her life. She couldn't help it. The experience left me wondering how we did decide to make the fateful climb in the first place......

Chapter 11. "Deciding to Climb Kilimanjaro"

Travel anticipation was always an aphrodisiac for Mary and me, most powerfully in our "second marriage". The germ of an idea would grab us, we'd do some research, sketch out the "what ifs," and start to get excited. At year's end we would sit and let ourselves dream about places we'd love to discover. We set three, five, and ten year goals, and I wrote them down. In 1996 Mary said "wouldn't it be cool to climb Mount Kilimanjaro with the kids? It's way too early now, they're only 11, 13, and 16 for heaven's sake." I wrote it down, putting it in the 10 year, "way out there" category, and promptly forgot about it. Funny things happen once these goals take root in our minds. Jim Rohn, the well respected author of Exceptional Living, would say once a goal is written down, the mind subconsciously prepares for an opportunity to achieve it. In late 2004, eight years later, a notice came in the mail that the Appalachian Mountain Club was hosting a seminar on their new Mount Kilimanjaro climb at the Explorer's Club in Manhattan. Mary turned to me with a twinkle in her eye, "wasn't that on our goal list a few years back?" Aha. Opportunity was knocking.

At the Explorer's Club, a veritable magnet for those afflicted with the adventurer's gene, we found our imaginations ignited. Mary, Trevor, and I walked down the dark wood paneled halls, surrounded by elephant tusks, pith helmets and photographs of exotic animals and dead explorers. "You can't just join this club," I explained to Trevor, "it's by invitation only." "Can't you just feel the ghosts of Livingston and Sir Edmund Hillary sitting down over there in the corner with a snifter of cognac?" Mary mused breathlessly.

A veteran mountain climber named Wes Krause painted for us a picture of what it would be like to mount the largest free-standing peak in the world, the tallest on the African continent. "How many of you in the room have climbed to 5,000 feet?" Most hands went up. "How many to 10,000 feet?" Wes asked. Many fewer, only a handful left. "How many to 15,000 feet?" None. "Well," he said, "if you take the challenge to summit Big Mama and see the sunrise, you can say you made it to 19,340 feet." We were swept away. There were details to work out, certainly, but I think the decision came that night.

Matt Viemeister is a world championship caliber natural body builder and strength trainer. In June, six months before the climb up Kilimanjaro, I presented myself at his gym. "Hello, Matt," I began, "I am 53 years old, out of shape, just had my hernia repaired one month ago, ruptured my right Achilles tendon eleven months ago, and I'm climbing to the top of Mount Kilimanjaro at over 19,000 feet in six months. You need to get me ready. Where do we start?" Matt's a tough guy, no doubt, but his jaw dropped a little, and his face paled. "Say that again?" he murmured, thinking to himself "what the hell kind of referrals is Dr. Naidoo (our mutual surgeon) sending me?" Matt gamely agreed to an assessment and took me on. Mary soon joined as well, each of us enduring three or four sessions a week of lunges, wind sprints, squats, leg presses and assorted other cardio and strength torture. Today he will say "I remember trying to simulate oxygen deprivation by forcing you and Mary through bursts of demanding cardio exercise. I felt bad watching you guys bent over, white-faced and nauseous." Little did we know we'd both be feeling the same way above 10,000 feet on Kilimanjaro. Nevertheless, we needed the conditioning. After Matt's ministrations, we felt we were ready, at least physically.

We got down to brass tacks at the beautiful Groton, Massachusetts home of Steve and Debbie Pittman a few weeks before our departure for Tanzania. There was a steely look of determination in Steve's eye when he welcomed us, and we soon learned why. "I was all set to go on the first Kilimanjaro climb last year, but just before we left I fell off a ladder and pulled the quad muscle clean off my right knee. What a bummer," he explained in his New England accent, "but I rehabilitated the crap out of it for months, and now I'm good to go!" His wife Debbie was genuinely enthusiastic, too.

We were here to pick up our Slumberjack subzero mummy sleeping bags and receive a day-by-day climb briefing. We would be transitioning, in one week on the mountain, from tropical rainforest climate to heather to the alpine zone to the equivalent of the freezing, lifeless surface of the moon atop Kilimanjaro. To be prepared for those challenges, the following items would be required: hand warmers, hot water bottles, Diamox for mountain altitude sickness (AMS), Cipro for infections, Tylenol for headaches, Pepto for nausea, Immodium for diarrhea, huge water bottles, and Personal Urinary Devices (for peeing in our pup tents at night in the freezing cold). Gulp. Poor Mary, physically and emotionally spent from the intense preparations, conked out on the couch for 15 minutes just after the briefing began. We chuckled nervously, but everyone knew the exhaustion she was feeling.

One clear message came through: this climb will not be a walk in the park. "Climbing Mount Kilimanjaro will test your limits and provoke your doubts, and you may not make it," stated one of the guides, bluntly. In contrast to the more popular "Coca Cola" route up Kilimanjaro, attempted by thousands every year (so named for the ubiquitous soda cans strewn on the trail by thoughtless climbers), which allows only four days to the summit, our AMC journey was designed to reach the top in seven days. "Many climbers trying the Coca Cola trail under prepare, suffer acclimation problems, and roughly 60% turn back, unsuccessful," the guide explained. There have been a few deaths on the route, we learned, mostly from Acute Mountain Sickness (lack of oxygen to the brain). While our organizers were purposefully allowing another three full days to acclimate to the altitude, they were also providing a portable hyperbaric chamber just in case. "If any of you shows signs of AMS at high altitude, we will place you in the chamber for 30 minutes, re-pressurize and re-oxygenate you, and then hustle you down the mountain to a hospital, pronto." I looked at Mary. She shook her head, "Please God, don't let that happen to my family or me."

Question time came. "How cold will it be?" "How rough is the terrain?" "What is the food like?" "How likely is it we will be sick?" "What other illnesses, besides AMS, could necessitate evacuation?" "How would you get us down, just in case?" The measured responses were firm, and not misleadingly comforting. The current Executive Director of AMC and a veteran of the first AMC Kilimanjaro summit last year, Andy Falender, rose to speak to us. A wonderful guy, Andy spoke from experience. "You are embarking on the adventure of a lifetime," he smiled. Then his face became serious. "The last full day of climbing, up a long, vertical breach of rock and snow, culminating in a short, sleepless, shivering, vomit-filled, headache-ridden night in a tent pitched on a glacier," he paused, "will be the worst day of your life." Thud. Mary glanced at me, eyes wide with fright. "The next day, after seeing the life-altering sunrise over the clouds atop magical Mount Kilimanjaro, skating down the other side, shedding layer after layer as the warmer and thicker air fills your lungs and brings euphoria," Andy paused again, "will be the best day of your life." Now Mary's smile widened into a grin. I felt like cheering. Wow, it would be a Dickensian adventure: the best of days, the worst of days.

In the last days before we took off for Africa, I know we each fulminated in our own way, but Mary was the most vocal and up front. She called her sisters in California and our family attorney to be clear they understand her intentions "in case we didn't make it back." I'd never heard her so worried before a trip. Son John overheard one of these conversations, and it jolted him. He wrote in his journal about the uneasiness "wow, this is serious." Mary was manic in her preparations, always rushing to get it all done, checking lists over and over. It was a metaphor for her life, those last few years. "Let's squeeze these trips in," she would chirp, "before our knees give out on us." I knew her worries about Alzheimer's and intestinal maladies as well. She confided in her friends her misgivings, but before they could ask "why are you doing this?" she would smile brightly and assure them "the adventure will be great. I love traveling with my family." The morning before we flew to Kilimanjaro International Airport, our 12 year old cranky calico cat was on our bed waiting for Mary to awake. As her eyes fluttered, the cat struck with her claws, badly scratching Mary's eyelid, requiring stitches. "Guys, this is bad," she warned us, on her way to the emergency room, "I'm afraid you may have to go on without me." That prospect made us all shiver, but the doctor sewed her up and pronounced her "good to go." This was only the first of several chances we all had to bail out, to miss "the adventure of a lifetime" on Mount Kilimanjaro.

If Mary had any sense of what was to transpire in the next eight days, she gave no indication, at least to me. She did not believe in predestination. She did subscribe to the notion that mediums can contact the dead, and she participated in several. After Mary passed, her sister Shirley asked her psychic pal Julie to make contact with her. The conversation was lively and touching until Shirley asked "Mare, did you have any fore-knowledge of what was coming? Is there pre-destination?" Mary's answer came back instantly and unequivocally, "Hell, no, Shirley. That's a pile of horseshit! If I'd known, I never would have gone to Africa. The last thing I would ever want would be to leave the people I love most: Scott, Trevor, Becky and John." When I ventured to see Mary with the help of a medium, seven months after the accident, she would have more amazing things to say.....

Chapter 12. "Mary Lou Speaks"

For months in the first half of 2006 I waited patiently for Mary to come to me, speak to me, touch my heart somehow. She had come to her friends and to her sister and to the psychics, but not to me. Julie, the California medium and friend of Shirley, posited that "when the one left behind on earth so desperately needs a vision contact, if the departed one complies, then the earthbound one can remain stuck, craving another contact." That made sense to me. I felt in my heart that Mary wanted me to move on, to live my life, to not be caught in a morose morass of missing her. Might she have been helping me move on by not appearing? Who knows...

Jim Fargiono is a quiet, understated legend in eastern Long Island, New York. A soft-spoken, unpretentious gentleman, Jim is so gifted as a medium his waiting list was eleven months long when Mary died. A friend gave up her July 12, 2006 appointment so I could take her place. For you skeptics this is important - Jim had no way of knowing I was attending that session and no way to prepare. I drove to Quogue with the usual trepidations: "what if Mary doesn't show up? What if there is bad news about the kids or my dad or my health?" I wasn't completely sold on the idea of contacting the dead, so I decided to keep my answers monosyllabic if possible, so as not to offer any helpful clues. I also came with a tape recorder and transcription equipment. What happened in the next hour I was completely unprepared for.

Pleasantries aside, Jim opened the session at ten in the morning, and the first to appear was my mother Ellie, who sent her love out to her husband Quentin, my dad. I was impressed Jim got both names exactly right. Then his eyes lit up and he said "Who's Mary? She's here. She just cut right in front of me. This was a very, very fast passing. She's laughing about it, but she's telling me there was no plan, no preparation for it. She's thanking you (Scott) and saying lots of people have to go through heartache, headache and physical pain, but she says she died being happy. She keeps apologizing to you (Scott) and smiling, 'Quite a trip.' She has a good sense of humor. She is so humorous about this whole thing. She just turned this into a little cartoon sketch. She's rolling down the mountain. Do you understand? She's telling me they put a roadblock in her way. She absolutely loves you, she needs you to know that. She's around the four of you in the family. There are three children? Two boys and a girl? She keeps telling me, in her very biased opinion, they are all very beautiful. She tells you again how much she loves you (Scott) and she doesn't want you to feel guilty about what happened."

"Were you on vacation?" Jim asked, without pausing. "She keeps telling me 'we were finally at a point where we could enjoy life, and look what happened!' She's throwing her hands up. She's coming across very happy. She's saying she understands the heartache it caused. She's very clear. She keeps saying she would do it all over again. And hope for a better result. She keeps talking about the roadblock. And saying 'don't feel guilty.' She's getting all soft and teary. I feel her tears. She doesn't want you to feel it was in any way your fault. She just smiled and said 'unless he was standing above her stomping'."

When I got the chance I asked about Mary's last moments before she passed, about our kids, about my father, who Jim did not know was recently diagnosed with cancer, and about our plans to dispense her ashes. I had been tortured about the ashes for six months; do I spread them or keep them? Do I give half to the California family? Keep them for a memorial bench somewhere? I gave Jim no idea of my machinations or of the details of our plan. Here's what Mary told him about our plans to distribute the ashes: "She's telling me 'out in the open air.' Was she this funny when she was here?" he chuckled. "She just went like this (licking his finger and testing the breeze) and said 'check the wind first.' She keeps showing me gorgeous scenery and telling me the mountain you're talking about didn't get burned down yet. Is there plenty of water there? She's saying something about being comfortable on top with a view of the water. About making the climb itself, she doesn't want you (Scott) to make yourself nuts, to stress yourself out about it. Do your kids literally climb also? But she's telling me only two want to. The older one does not want to climb. She is so funny, she's showing me the older one with straps on, being towed up by a helicopter. Let him take the easy way up. He will stress too much. We both know how he makes himself crazy, which makes the whole family crazy. Don't push him. Can't force it on him. He's a good, good boy. Then she smiles and says 'well, he's not a boy anymore, but a man.'"

The idea that I needed to say goodbye, and let go of Mary, so she could go about her business in the afterlife was offered by our Ayurvedic medical advisor, Dr. Albrecht Heyer. I resisted the idea. I didn't want to let go, so I asked Mary, through Jim, if I should. "She just waved her hand and said 'pfffft' (no way!) With all due respect, the doc is taking this all too clinically. She has her hand on her hip, saying 'I'm gonna have a talk with this one.' She doesn't want you to feel like you can't reach her. It's the opposite of what Dr. H said. She understands his reasons for wanting closure, but she feels I have it with Mary. She's freeing you (Scott) so you can move your life forward. She doesn't want to talk about this, but she knows you (Scott) are still young enough to have a wife. You shouldn't feel guilty about the opportunity to wine and dine. She says Doc is worried about finality and closure and moving on. What's the difference if you two keep talking? She's not holding you back, and you're not holding her back. She just sarcastically wanted to know 'when was the last time you stopped her from doing something she wanted to do?' She says the docs sometimes live from the books too much. Life is about having a spirit that is free to move, free to roam, and untrapped. Her life is all about this."

At this point Jim paused. We had covered a lot of ground with Mary. He looked at me and said he was surprised we were able to "hold her in" this long – 40 minutes. According to Jim, spirits usually sign off after only a few minutes of contact. Mary still had more to say. "She is very insistent, if she couldn't talk or didn't want to talk, she wouldn't be here this long." Mary talked some more about this amazing "conduit" that she never knew about, and she cautioned me that I would never be able to be aware of her presence. She giggled and said she couldn't wait to see her grandchildren because they can see her and converse with her. Now, it was time for Mary to be moving on. "She's telling me she knows you (Scott) always loved her. Well, maybe not this one time..." My eyes widened in protest. "No, no," Jim continued, "She knows you always loved her. She's just busting your chops. She keeps repeating how much she loves you and the family. She's very clear about this: she doesn't want to have her passion for life and her independence on some level – and she is very emotional at this point – to be mistaken for not loving you and the kids to the fullest. She did love you with all her heart. And you have to know that, OK?" At this juncture, both Mary and I were crying together, but in separate dimensions.

A month later we four made the trip out to Yosemite National Park to climb Half Dome as Mary wished, and send her ashes into the beautiful valley. Sure enough, as Mary had predicted, Trevor could not bring himself to climb. I know he wanted to, but, after his near-death motorcycle accident a few years back and our brush with death on Kilimanjaro, he has been understandably reluctant to place his life in jeopardy. The climb was arduous. I fell behind the family crowd, much as Mary had on her Half Dome climb. I caught my breath at one point, got goose bumps and looked at the red back pack I was carrying – it just dawned on me the pack was the one Mary wore on Kilimanjaro. On the dangerous smooth spine of Half Dome both of my legs cramped up, but I drank a liter of water, pushed through the panic, and joined the group on top. It was a calm day, clear as could be, at the cliff. I dutifully licked my finger to check to wind, as Mary had reminded me through Jim Fargiono, we all shed a little tear, and then we each dumped a little bag of ashes and flower petals into the gentle breeze that carried them to the valley and beyond.

The next day we found a glorious green shimmering pool on a back country hike and performed a more private ceremony. Placing a last bit of Mary's ashes and some of her mom, Amy's, into the little pool, Becky, Shirley, a few others and I cried as the gentle currents accepted the offered remains, and they became part of the pool. As we said goodbye again, we knew Mary would be happy to be with her mom in this sweet quiet place. Later that day I read parts of Jim Fargiono's transcript as a message from Mary. Every single listener, from age 16 to 60+, was speechless, tearful and ever so grateful to hear their Mary speak again.

A week after we returned home from California, I read reports of a significant forest fire in Yosemite which cut off the approach to Half Dome. Remembering Mary's words, "the mountain you're talking about didn't get burned down yet," gave me chills.

As ecstatic as I was at hearing from my feisty, passionate soul mate at the medium's session, I continued to grind over some ideas rattling around in my head. How could I possibly survive the loneliness of my empty home when the children scattered in September? I knew Mary forgave me for not coming to her on the mountain as she was dying, but why did I do that? And, could I forgive myself? She was the love of my life! And, weren't there circumstances in that last week of her life, on Mount Kilimanjaro, which would have allowed us to avoid this nightmare? Couldn't I have done something? I miss Mary so. Why did this have to happen?

Chapter 13. "On Kilimanjaro: No Turning Back"

It is now December 28, 2005 and we are at Kilimanjaro International Airport. It's 10pm. and we are exhausted but ready for "the adventure of a lifetime." Mary is beautiful. Her face betrays none of the trepidation or worries she has felt in the past weeks. She has done what she can to prepare. In another hour we arrive at the Mount Meru acclimation camp at 7000 feet. Who knows how many miles away from home we are now? We crawl into our canvas tent cabins after midnight and try to sleep. That's not happening, but it's not big deal. "We'll sleep for sure tomorrow night," we think.

The next day, in our first full day in Africa, we hike up another 2000 feet and receive some last minute preparation advice during a meal in the large canvas mess tent. On the hike John and Becky get a little scare. John queries Kambona how many times he had summited Kilimanjaro. In his clipped, matter-of-fact tone, the confident trek leader replies "one oh two" and does not smile. Becky's eyes get as big as saucers. "One or two times only? Are we placing our lives in the hands of a novice leader?" she thinks to herself. Seeing their confusion, Kambona clarifies "one hundred and two. This climb will be number one hundred and three." John laughs, relieved, and Becky's smile says she is also.

The second night does not go well. "Last night was a crisis for me," I write in my journal. Trying to maximize my chances for some much needed sleep this second night, I take a codeine painkiller at 10pm, and then toss and turn until 1:30am. I play the game "A, my name is Adam and I'm an attorney from Alabama" five times through the alphabet in my head. Frustrated to the max that I cannot sleep, I wake up Mary and tell her I am panicked. She suggests I take two more Tylenol and she will give me a back rub. She caresses me gently for what seems an eternity. I feel loved and relaxed, but the lights will not go out, I still can't sleep. Mary even offers to make love with me. For the first time in our 30 year romance, I decline. She finally rolls over and falls into a fitful sleep. At 3am or so I have had enough, so angry am I at my body for refusing to acclimate. I decide I will simply pass on the climb and wait for the family in the hotel at the bottom of the mountain. This decision relieves me, but not enough to allow sleep. At 5:30am. my thrashing around wakes Mary. I explain my plan to bail out. She rises on one elbow and says "Scott, I have to talk to you like a Dutch uncle. You <u>must</u> climb this mountain. You never give up. Your kids and I need you. You are the leader of this family. We are five sticks bundled together, unbreakable." I choke up. Mary smiles, "also, if you miss out on this adventure, you will be such a miserable S.O.B. that I won't be able to live with you. It's settled." And she rolls over again. I remember thinking "God. I love this woman."

December 30th starts the Kilimanjaro climb. We begin at the rainforest staging area which is 6,700 feet in altitude. The six dozen strong young local guys check their duffels and packs, grab ours and take off, a brightly colored, upbeat army. The fifteen of us are apprehensive, all geared up, but I remember thinking that Steve and Debbie seem confident, more than ready to go. They have prepared for this trip twice, and Steve seems like an authority to all of us first-timers. We will be able to rely on his strength and wisdom out on the trail. About an hour or so into the first leg of the hike, in the moist, sticky rainforest, I am following Steve. We are all in single file on the narrow path. A misty precipitation is making the red clay trail slippery, I notice. Suddenly the path ahead dips down sharply. I lengthen my poles, as we were instructed, to brace my descent down this slope. I am wary because of my Achilles history and need all the help I can get. Like my children, however, Steve is not using his poles. I watch as he plants his left leg at the lip of the drop off. Now things move in slow motion. His right leg, surgically repaired and strong as iron, slips out from his next placement, leaving his full body weight supported entirely by the unrepaired left leg. In excruciating slow motion, I watch his leg buckle under the unexpected weight and give out with a sickening pop. He has severed the quadriceps muscle from the knee on his "good" leg. Steve crumples onto the slippery red clay. Kambona swiftly cuts and strips a straight sapling and splints Steve's leg. Watching Kambona perform emergency medicine on the knee, it hits us instantly that Steve's climb is finished. Lightning has struck twice. Debbie sobs as she hugs us all goodbye. Steve is stoic as he is lifted and half-carried back up the trail to the truck that will take him to the hospital. Kambona walks with Debbie. Now we are 13. It is only the first 90 minutes of our Kilimanjaro adventure. We are rattled, not sure what it all means.

In the next four hours we hike to our first camp in the Montane Forest at 9,000 feet. Before dinner I feel sleepy, and Mary is shivering with an oncoming fever so she crawls into her Slumberjack bag and tries to warm up. Dinner revives me somewhat, but not Mary. She goes to bed exhausted. Diarrhea visits her at 4:30am., and she awakes to panic. A little wardrobe accident messes her up and lowers her spirits. "I don't think I can do this," she sniffles. I clean her up, sooth her, and assure her the medics will fix her up tomorrow. She nods back into a fitful sleep. Kambona gives her Cipro and Immodium in the morning, and by noon she is a new woman. "This isn't going to beat me," she vows. I am relieved and proud of her.

Now it's Saturday, New Year's Eve, and the expedition planners have prepared a celebratory dinner with decorations on the mess tent, but Mary is relapsing, and neither of us feels up for a party of any sort. At dinner, Kambona implores all of us to eat twice as many calories as we normally consume at home. "You need to warehouse energy for the hardest, last two days of the climb, when even hikers who feel normal don't want to eat," he says. Mary and I are already having trouble choking down food. With her typical determination, Mary gamely eats bread with butter, rich peanut soup, French fries, battered fried tilapia and vegetables in butter sauce. That night, outside our little tent, she regurgitates all of it, three or four times. Mary loses not only tonight's New Year's Eve dinner, but it seems like her paltry lunch and breakfast as well, and much of the liquids. I am alarmed and fetch Kambona. He asks if she has a headache. "No," she says forlornly. She is still taking Cipro and Immodium. "Let's see how you feel tomorrow," Kambona says, showing no outward signs of concern. It is only Day 2.

During the wee hours that night Mary sobs in my arms. She has decided to go back down to Arusha in the morning. "I feel like such a wuss giving up like this, but I just can't take it any more," she whimpers. I patiently explain "Honey, no one who has birthed three children, endured two weeks on the desert at Outward Bound, jumped tandem out of a Cessna at 10,000 feet, and climbed to 11,000 feet on Mount Kilimanjaro could ever be called a wuss." She stops crying, "I guess you're right." We agree to sort out her warmer weather clothes for Arusha and get ready her passport and money. I accept her anguish, and do not give her the Dutch Uncle speech. Later I will be grateful for not changing her mind. She needed relief from the physical agony. I seriously offered to join her in going down to Arusha. I was miserable too, in the throes of a week-long headache and fever. "No, you must continue on. You are the leader. I will be OK," she says bravely.

New Year's morning Mary awakes sad, but determined.

She informs Kambona and Paul, our AMC guide, and then tells Trevor, Becky and John "kids, I'm going back down to the hotel. I will wait for you," she says, tears streaming. She repacks her kit and gives her Slumberjack to Virginia and other items to those who need them. Kambona considers her decision and lets her know "there is no road close to this camp. The closest take out point is at our next camp, Shira 2. You must come up with us one more day, spend the night, and we'll see how you feel." I suspect Kambona does not want to let Mary go. Maybe it was the sight of magnificent Big Mama back lit by the brilliant morning sun, or maybe it was her destiny. Who know? Mary gracefully accepts Kambona's logic, and pulls on her hiking boots one more time.

That Sunday Mary is flagging but determined to make it to the takeout point at Shira 2. The brilliant morning sun gives way to mid-day clouds and cold fog. Our spirits sink, and our feet get heavier. My head aches, pounding like a jackhammer in the steeper parts of the trail. "Drink water, drink water," Kambona urges us, to stave off the headaches caused by the altitude. It's not working for me, despite liter upon liter of flavored water. It seems all I do is urinate, twelve times at night and at least that number during the day. I'm sick of it. That night the chills get me. I remember shaking so violently for ten seconds, then calming for 50 seconds, only to repeat the process in the ensuing minutes. Even in her depleted state, Mary attempts to comfort me. For fifteen minutes she massages my temples. The chills and violent shaking finally subside, and the headache simmers down from a ten on the pain Richter scale to maybe a four. Mary even offers to make love to me. Considering we haven't bathed in many days and were disgusting under our many layers of clothes, I count it the sweetest, most generous offer I ever got. For the second time in our 30 year romance, I decline again. "She has been the best mate I could imagine. I owe her a ton," I write later in my journal. Maybe it was the nursing she gave me, or a burst of energy she got from some unknown source, but when Kambona came to her the next morning to check on her, Mary told him "I'm good to go another day." She's not going to leave the group after all. Maybe Kambona was right.

Journal entry, January 3, 2006: "Another brutal day for me. I've had a fucking headache for days now – worst while climbing, using the mountaineering step (step, breathe, step, breathe, etc.). Pounding. Nasty. Up at camp I just want to crawl in the bag and die." The stress is showing now. Mary is rebounding some, finding reserves of strength she maybe hasn't accessed since Outward Bound. The mountain is cloudy now and bone-chillingly cold. Hot water bottles are issued to keep our feet from frostbite in the Slumberjacks. I am taking a double dose of Diamox, so my fingers and toes tingle constantly. After we arrive at camp I experience explosive diarrhea and ruin a second pair of underwear. Very humbling. My body is weakening, I realize. I can feel it, and I doubt I can physically make it. The specter of AMS haunts me. Kambona is aware but keeps his distance. My kids pull me aside, "one more bad day, Dad. You got this." Tomorrow we face the Western Breach, a 4,200 foot hike, but 2,500 feet elevation gain, which will take between eight and ten hours to the glacier camp, a few more hours from the summit. At an excruciatingly slow pace I calculate a roughly 60% grade, making maybe 400 to 500 feet of progress along the ground per hour. The math takes me forever. My brain is very slow.....

5 am. January 4, 2006. "Mahning, good mahning," comes the gentle wake up greeting from the porter. I am up already, mole skinning my ruined toes for the final push up Mount Kilimanjaro's Western Breach. "The worst day of your life," I recalled Andy Falender telling us, followed by a three hour hike in the dark, a glorious sunrise, and then the euphoric run back down into thicker, warmer air. "I can do this," I willed my body. Still have chills and headache, my old friends. I was only up eight times last night. My diarrhea alerted me in enough time to don the mountain booties and pick my way to the toilet tent across the frozen moonscape, littered with rocks so sharp they seem to have come out of Big Mama's volcanic belly yesterday. The tents glimmered in the light from my headlamp. There were ice crystals in the tent's air. Mary was bundled completely except for a slit open for her nose. I wake her. She's groggy and weak, but she rises to perform a Sammis family tradition. Mary picks her way over to the boys' tent and sings "Happy Birthday" to Trevor in his Slumberjack bag. He is 26 today. Trevor remembers Mary was "pumped" for the day. She smiles at her oldest and asks him "How are we gonna

top <u>this</u> for your birthday next year?"

By now, at 16,000 feet plus, the altitude is making even the children stupid. Becky and Trevor feel groggy. Becky has trouble tying her boot laces and thinks "why am I going so slow?" Trevor feels the grogginess is novel, almost like being inebriated. I remember casting around the tiny tent in the beam of my headlamp thinking "where the hell is that other sock?' Focus, focus. Mary is out of the tent before me. She finds Kambona and takes his hand. "Thank you. Without you I wouldn't be here,' Mary says. Soon, before 6am, as Kambona has requested, we are all equipped, dressed and ready. I remember nervously taking a mental inventory of the five of us. "Whew," I sigh to myself, "at least we're all here together. We can climb this nasty last piece of the mountain side by side."

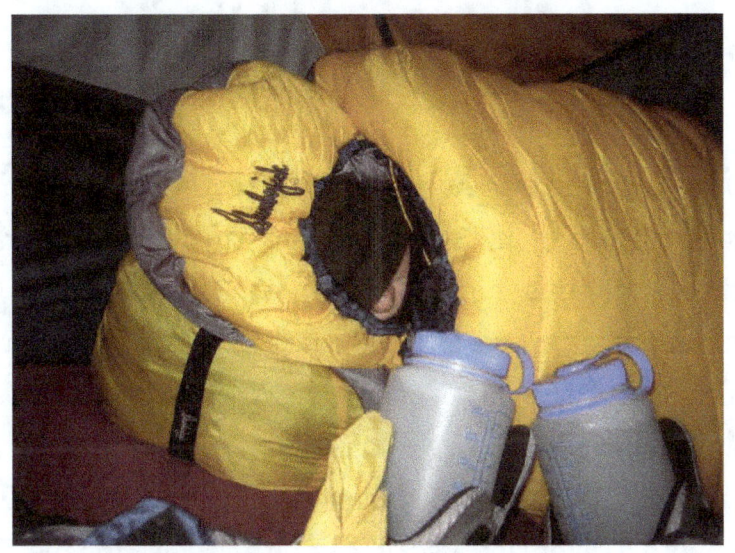

Chapter 14. "Abandonment and Guilt, A Nasty Combination"

After Yosemite in late August 2006, Trevor and Becky and I stayed with John in Santa Barbara to help him find an apartment for his next semester at Santa Barbara City College. By the time we left to fly back to New York, John had nothing solid in the way of apartment leads, but he kept a stiff upper lip about it. If he felt half as bad as I did, leaving him there alone, his heart must have been torn to bits. Flying home with Trevor and Becky was bittersweet for me, for I knew in a few days, the darkest day of my life was coming: I had already named it Black Labor Day. Trevor had to work before Labor Day so he trained and bussed down to DC as soon as we arrived in Huntington. He had been coming and going from NY to DC for years since he graduated University of Richmond. As hard as it was to see him go, it didn't seem as traumatic to me. Becky saw some friends, collected her apartment stuff, packed her little red Hyundai Elantra, and stood before it, tears streaming down her face. It was time to go. She hated leaving me as much as I hated seeing her go. It was the right thing to do. Life goes on. "I love you, Dad, take care of yourself and Niko. I'll see you soon," she sniffled. "I love you sweetie," I choked, "call me every ten minutes, you hear?"

She nodded her head, buckled her seat belt and drove slowly away.

What is it about abandonment fears, exactly? I knew this day was coming. I worried about it for months. When it was finally real, the emotion still brought me to my knees. I walked unhurriedly back to face the red front door of our house. I talked to Mary, "well, here it is, the day we waited for, the Empty Nest is finally here. But you aren't! How could you do this to me? To us? You have to be here! I can't do this alone!"

The red front door squeaked its familiar squeak as it opened and closed behind me. I sleepwalked through the blackness. It was a magnificent bright blue September day, but I did not notice. I walked through every room in the house, trailing tears, finally plopping myself in an Adirondack chair Trevor and I had built for the back deck. The sobs came, the tears flowed. If I was so upset here in the bright sunshine, "how will I face tonight in the dark alone?" My Old Friend the Blues was here, and this time it felt like he was moving in permanently. I never remember it being this black before. The hole was deep, and I didn't lift a finger to crawl out. "Go ahead, take your best shot," I dared the blackness. I think I cried for 45 minutes, but it might have been three weeks. Niko the dog left me alone on the deck. I finally realized the crying had stopped- maybe the tear ducts were empty. I was aware Niko had returned, looking at me sadly, head down. It was over. A little glimmer of hope popped up, a sliver of euphoria. "Whew.

That was bad, but it didn't kill me. I'm still here." What to do next? I hear a motorcycle roaring in the distance. Maybe I can outrun this, just keep moving? No, we must attend the grief, face up to it.

"Let's do something bold," I talked to myself, "something I've been dreading since January, something inconceivable previously. Let's put Mary's clothes in boxes to give to her sisters and to charity." Right. Up the stairs we clumped, Niko and I, and into her closet I ventured. At this point, I'm expecting My Old Friend to kick my ass again, but he seems to have left the building. Sure enough, I filled four boxes, leaving only Mary's wedding dress and my favorite pieces of her clothing that smelled like her. As I'm sorting, my rational side spoke: "Mary hated most of these clothes, never felt comfortable in them, preferring the tried and true denim and black tops. The stuff she hated can go." Good job, we're on a roll, I figured. What next? How about going through the picture book of Mary Lou's life that brother Gary assembled and I had banished deep into a drawer? Hell yes, I said to myself, again daring My Old Friend to reappear. Page by page, I soaked in the images of Mary Lou, from impossibly cute childhood through sassy adolescence and exuberant adulthood. The wedding photos nearly got to me, but I made it through. The last I remember of that day was riding my motorcycle out of the driveway, just to be moving somewhere.

Black Labor Day left its mark on me, however. I had found

wonderful Dee Margolis, a family counselor at the Family Service League in Huntington around the six month anniversary of the accident on Kilimanjaro, at about the time my father Quentin received his first cancer diagnosis. Dee and I had met a few times during the summer, but I was gone a lot, and we were still in the familiarization stage. Black Labor Day told me it was time to get serious.

At our intake meeting that summer, Dee asked me "what are you most afraid of?" My first answer was "the kids are struggling," but she didn't accept that. She wanted to know about me. "OK," I tried again, "I worry that I can't handle September, afraid I'll crawl into a fetal position." Dee persisted, "What are you really worried about?" "I want another wonderful relationship, but I can't let Mary go, and it won't work unless I work through this completely," I confessed. "Right you are," she agreed.

"Are you angry?," she continued. "Yes, I'm angry that she left me and won't be here to share September and beyond with me. She was supposed to be here when the nest emptied out. Now I'm solo. It's not fair," I whined. "Are you still in shock?" Dee queried. "Yes, I believe so," I replied, "It feels like it happened yesterday." "What will you do with the ashes? she asked. "I haven't figured that out yet," I admitted. "You don't want to let her go, to say goodbye," Dee said. "Scott, Mary will always be a part of you, almost a part of your DNA. You won't lose that even if you marry many times."

Dee: "Do you feel guilty about surviving?"

Scott: "No."

Dee: "Do you feel guilty about not touching or speaking to her?"

Scott: "Yes," but it was an unconvincing affirmative, lacking depth or emotion.

Dee: "You were in complete shock and the children were holding her. There was nothing you could have done."

Scott: "I took a picture."

Dee: "You wanted to capture her, not let her get away. My friend, you can't wrap up memories neatly, so don't say goodbye yet. There are many layers of grief. You will have ups and downs, advances and setbacks. It may take a year or years, and you can't hurry the process. You will have to integrate the loss into your life. When you think of Mary in the future, the memory must be filled with love, not with the loss. We have our work cut out for us.

See you next week."

Dee and I worked on a variety of issues that fall, after Black Labor Day, but she did not revisit my guilt about not saying goodbye to Mary on the mountain. She knew it was there, but she needed to let our trust develop enough so we could tackle it without provoking my defenses. So instead we talked about my children's refusal to engage in helpful grief counseling, my decision to sell the family business I'd nurtured for 25 years, my father's diagnosis with deadly Cancer of Unknown Primary Origin, which would wind up taking his life next August, or my own attempts at dating, which crashed and burned. The kids and I flew to California for Christmas with Mary's extended family. I forgot to bring presents for my children, inexplicably. Trevor was hurt by my oversight, and told me so. They refused to talk about Mary or Africa. I felt estranged from them. The sale of the business was consummated on January 3rd 2007. I remember thinking "I'll be financially OK, but my days as a business-owner are over." My dad's cancer disappeared under treatment with Avastin, but reappeared in January, devastating all of the family's optimism. One perfectly delightful lady wound up shaking her head at my inability to commit to the simplest of relationships. Dee discussed each of these situations calmly and deliberately. She waited for the right moment to raise the issue of my guilt on the mountain.

By the third week of January, 2007, some good things were happening – John had decided to come home from Santa Barbara, and all three children had agreed to see Dee individually to get help – and Dee knew it was time to bring up the guilt. She began gently, "Do you shy away from people in pain? Is it hard to look at suffering? What was it like for you to see Mary was struck on the mountain? You couldn't face it. It would have been easy to deny that an incomprehensible thing was happening. Scott, do you have guilt about not going to Mary on Mount Kilimanjaro?" The full realization of the enormity of my guilt hit me like a ton of bricks. I gulped "yes," and couldn't speak further. "Are you ready to try to understand your feelings and resolve them?" Through tearful eyes I nodded. It was time.

Dee recommended I read a book on Somatic Experiencing called <u>Waking</u> <u>the Tiger</u>: <u>Healing Trauma</u> by Peter A. Levine. She knew I am a believer in Darwin's Theory of Evolution and a serious student of how animal behavior can help us to understand our own. The book starts by discussing the altered state called the "immobility" or "freezing" response animals use in addition to the flight or fight responses when facing an overwhelming threat. Also known as "playing possum," it allows prey to not suffer if they are attacked, but more importantly, if the predator doesn't kill them right away, to shake off the trauma later and escape. I was intrigued. I only read as far as Chapter 6, "In Trauma's Reflection," to discover the first step in Dr. Levine's healing process, which is to experience the "felt sense." For me, it was to close my eyes, completely relax, feel each and every part of my body, feel how the chair and floor make contact with my back and feet, etc., and let my mind come up with whatever images it wants to.

Rather than finish the book and thoroughly understand the processes and pitfalls, I dove right in. Sitting in an overstuffed blue chair in my den, safe at home in the quiet, I relaxed myself, and took a felt sense inventory of how each of my body parts was feeling. Slight back pain, right side, my left shoe too tight, neck a little stiff, heart rate low, but rising... My mind was clear until an image of a mountain top appeared, backlit. In the next instant I was back on Kilimanjaro, and the Volkswagen-sized boulder was careening down to the right of me. I felt my body go on full alert, muscles tensing. Some small boulders flew past on our left, incredibly fast, in my mind's eye. Now my heart rate and breathing are rapidly escalating. I detect the medium size rock coming right for me. Bam! I wake up abruptly from the felt sense experience before the killer rock gets to me, sweating, near panic. I refocus on the paint in the den, look out the windows to the backyard. My heart rate recovers, breathing stabilizes, I am OK. But, wow, was that ever real! The felt sense has the power to bring me back to the scene of the terror, the Western Breach of Mount Kilimanjaro.

I explained this to Dee and she cautioned me not to go further without guidance and help. "We humans don't release the pent up energy of the immobilizing trauma event as easily as animals. We don't just shake it off and move on with our lives. Animals don't have the luxury of nurturing the traumas and feeling depressed for years. The next predator is always lurking around the corner, and they need to be ready. We humans can retain the pent up energy for years, perhaps a lifetime," she said. I told her "I believe I was immobilized by the near-death experience I had on the mountain and by Mary's being struck and killed. I want to release the energy and heal myself." Dee cautioned "If you go about it the wrong way, all you will do is succeed in provoking the trauma again and again and driving it deeper into your psyche. Best case, you suffer the trauma all over again; worst case, you make it worse. Better to take it slow."

Sufficiently chastened by Dee's sage advice, I agreed to wait to proceed further. Anyway, John was home, I had sold the business, and my dad's relapse was happening. I had plenty to occupy myself. I could put aside the felt sense until I read the rest of Waking the Tiger. I would have plenty of time in February when I will fly to Jupiter, Florida to visit my dad, his wife and my sister. A couple of days of warmer weather and good company might provide me some clarity. "Who knows," I thought to myself, "maybe Mary will finally come to me a put my mind at ease."

Chapter 15. "Re-Imagining the Tragedy"

Delta flight 1748 left LaGuardia Airport on Thursday 2/22/07, headed for West Palm Beach, Florida, with me in aisle seat Row 35D, relaxed, anticipating a pleasant visit with Quentin, Marge and my sister Sue. After leveling off, I closed my eyes, aware of the jabbering flight attendants and the snack cart nearby. Peace came quickly, and soon I became aware of how Seat 35D was pressing on my legs, back and buttocks. I felt my shoes pinch my feet and the seat back bend my neck. An image formed in the blackness behind my eyelids of a grumpy woman with a severe frown which then morphed into a mountain rising in the sun. My heart palpitated slightly, my breathing shallowed, and my neck tightened imperceptibly. I felt the glimmer of a headache – the same Kilimanjaro headache I suffered for four days. I could feel the clammy balaclava, smell it, on my face, the bulky gloves, my right toe chafing in my boot, the clunky gaiters, the thick layers of clothes, now too hot, oppressive. I worry over the incredible insecurity of shifting rocks and gravel beneath me – one misstep and I could slip away down the mountain like the day I nearly plummeted to my death rock climbing with my buddies in California. I remembered that as a slow motion slide into open space, totally helpless, terrified. I now see streaks across my field of closed eyes vision, behind my eyelids. Are they missiles? What's coming? My head hurts. I feel mentally diminished, but happy to have stopped climbing. I now realize why Kambona pushed us hard to climb as high as possible. We started too late, he sensed the danger.... I also realize now both Mary and Betty were eager for this day, they wanted to engage it, to "get there," wherever that was.....They went together, gloriously, heroically.

The rumble happens, the rocks are coming. Despite my tenuous hold on the earth, I stand up to face the terror. "Bring it on!" I hear myself challenging, "Show me!" I want a chance to survive the test. My senses heighten to total alertness. My enfeebled brain, even as slow as it was, realizes how fast the rocks are coming - not like dodgeball in grade school which I loved -cannot wait until the last minute. Must recognize and move fast. Cannot wait. Here comes one, growing fast, right at me. "Move left, NOW!" I yell at myself. I twist, lean, dodge. Whoosh, it flies by. "Holy shit, that was close!" I am still standing. Whew. Breathe, gulp air. I am still standing. I am still standing. (A different part of my brain is aware I am shaking and sobbing, both in the dream and on the airplane in Seat 35D) Is it the joy that I'm not dead? Relief? I am still standing. "Come on, Fucker, what else you got?" I defy the mountain. I almost want another one. Is this the euphoria? Total sensory survival instinct on steroids. Pulling up resources, reactions that were previously unimaginable. A "Matrix"-like twist away. Suspend time, slow down the rock, speed up the twisting, evasive motion. Wow. I am still standing!

The rocks stop. Quiet. Tense muscles. Total alert. Breathing shallow. Eyes wide open on the mountain. Focus broadening to take in more than me and the attacking rocks. "Holy shit, Betty is dead!" Instant awareness that this has been a lethal attack. Look up ahead. Trevor OK, John OK, Becky OK. Oh NO, Mary is down, looks in pain. She was hit. Not dead, still alive. Must get to see, get closer......The flight attendant gently shakes me, the passenger in Seat 35D, a concerned look on her face. I am shaking and crying. "Are you OK, sir?" Bleary, refocusing, I nod and smile. She's relieved. So am I.

Thursday and Friday are enjoyable days in Jupiter, Florida. After dinner the second night I'm off to bed at midnight, a little tipsy. When I drink Jack Daniels I always guzzle water as well to mitigate the miserable feeling the next morning. At 3:10am. Saturday morning it's dark and quiet in the front bedroom of the 3rd floor condo. I have to arise to respond to Nature's call. I nestle back under the covers in the air conditioning, on my back, and relax. The images come again, clear as life....so do the feelings: my big toe throbs in the right hiking boot, my head pounds. The sticky balaclava, the sweaty clothes, the pin pricks of diamond light in my field of vision. The familiar icy dread fills my abdomen. The huge rock tumbles down to our right. The batch of smaller ones fly by us on the left. We are under attack.

The boulder with my name on it comes at me, this time in slow motion. It's bigger and I can see the grainy detail on its surface as it approaches, closer, closer. It fills my view space. BAM! I'm hit, down on the rocky ground. There's no pain, just surprise. I'm aware I'm not right. I start to float gently above the situation on the mountain. I look down on my unmoving body, crumpled. As I drift above, Kambona takes the pulse of the body and says "He's gone. Oh my God, he's gone. Go to the children!" The kids are crushed, white faced, sobbing, disbelieving. Mary is consumed with her battle for survival, unaware. "Holy shit," I think, "It happened. I'm gone." A vast sadness sets in. "What about the kids? What will happen to the kids?" I am moving higher. In a field of light, my mother Ellie is there, and other familiar faces. They are smiling. I feel a gladness, a warmth. But my brain rejects this outcome. "NO! NO! I must get back to the kids and Mary!"

Suddenly I'm back on Mount Kilimanjaro, the bombardment continues, and my rock is hurtling at me again, smaller this time. I am bobbing, weaving. It misses me, narrowly. The images meld, get confused. The message garbles. I feel iciness in my bowel as the rock passes, death missing me by inches. A shudder in my neck, a twinge of pain. I can see nothing more...... I awake from the death scenario and realize I am alive, I am lying in a bed in the third floor condominium of my father in Jupiter, Florida. As I peer out the window of the bedroom, a message comes softly but urgently: "Come outside. Come outside."

I dress in the dark, pulling on jeans and a tee shirt. Something awaits me in the dark outside. An answer? An experience? A message? A catharsis? Something bad? Calmly I find my cell phone, keys and journal, remove my NY drivers license from my wallet and slip it into my pocket. "If I get assaulted out there in the middle of the night, they won't get my wallet, but the authorities can ID my body." I insert my contact lenses in the bathroom,turn off the light, and leave the condo quietly.

Walking down the three flights of stairs, my senses are heightened. I notice every crack in the concrete, every spider on the wall. It is breezy, dark and fragrant. I see the red flowers are open. There is a beetle crawling slowly across a step. The clouds are dappling the sky, the light from the stanchions has a peculiar quality tonight, the leaves are moistened by the sprinklers. My eyes are drawn to an eastern planet. Is it Jupiter? I walk east, across the sandy, scrubby exercise course, toward the beach. I am aware of fear. Who is out after 3am on a Friday night? Will I need to run to escape? Is this the trauma/escape I need? The breeze is a little cool so I shiver briefly. Clouds mostly occlude the stars and planet. No moon is visible.

Past the dark lot I cross A1A and enter the public beach parking lot. I pass the concession building, the garishly lit Men's Room. A maintenance generator hums, still on duty. The pathway to the beach is overarched by mangrove trees, creating a dark tunnel, eerie. The fear persists. I am drawn to within ten yards of the ocean. I sit. "Should I sit facing the beach pathway to see if any bad guys approach?" No, I am here for a different reason. I put the fear in my pocket, face the ocean, and lie down in the sand, head on my journal. I look up at the bright star directly above. I am open, totally aware. The scudding clouds make it appear the universe is really moving tonight...

Sensing a receptiveness, I ask questions, of no one in particular. "Why am I here? Mary, are you there? Is Mary there?" "Yes," comes the message, again with no sound or image attached. The words simply appear in my consciousness. "Is she happy?" I continue. "Absolutely," the answer makes me smile. "Does she know I love her?" I query. "Yes, and she loves you, always will," to which I smile again. "What is my purpose? Do I have a purpose?" I question. "Seek. Search. Teach. You are a teacher," comes the message. "What should I teach?" I wonder. "The truth. Teach your truth. You will know it when you find it" explains the disembodied voice. "Who will teach me?" I venture. "You will know them when you meet them. You will know," assures the messenger. "Is my time here up?" I worry. "No" comes the answer, quick and sure. "When will my time be up?" I press. "In due time" counsels the mysterious messenger. "How will I know? Will I know when it's my time?" "Yes you will, when your time comes" the reply says. "Will it be a surprise?" "No" One final question, "Will you help me with my trauma?" "Yes," comes the answer, softly, gently. "Tonight?" I press. "If you wish. Stand up" comes the instruction.

I stand. The breeze seems to quicken. My eyes close. I am back on Mount Kilimanjaro. The shifting, treacherous surface of the Western Breach is now represented by the beach sand below me. I feel the heavy clothing, my knees are braced for whatever is coming. I look up the mountain and the rumble comes. I am riveted, my bowels ice, and my body begins to shake. The first giant rock crashes down to my right, splitting, hurtling down, fast, fast. My knees buckle. I start to shiver, quiver. Oh my God. Another rock hurtles past on the left. Now I know we are under attack. Shit, here comes the killer. I twist left, dodge, lean, escape. Whooooosh. Fuck! I'm now shaking like a leaf. Are there more? Whoa, that was close! I'm shaking, quaking. Quiet. Knees knocking, body quivering. Look to the right. Betty is quiet, feet facing down the mountain, turned around. Dead. I know it. I see the blood trail. Death is here. Slowly I turn to check on my family. One, two, three, moving. OK, whew! Thank God! Wait! Mary is down. No, No, No, No! Sobbing, wailing, screaming into the wind, "She can't be dying!!!" I know I must get to her!

Blindly, eyes still closed, staggering, I scramble across the few yards up to where Mary lies, struggling up the shifting surface. I don't care about losing my balance on the dangerous scrabble. I make it to her, I fall onto her body and hug her. She strokes my hair. I sob uncontrollably. "Mary, you can't leave me! I love you! I need you!" "I know you do," she says softly, "but it's OK, I'll be fine." I'm choked up, quaking, wracked with sobs. "How will I raise these kids without you?" I wail. "You will be fine. You will get help. I will be there for you," she soothes. "Don't leave me!" I repeat, insistently. "I must go. It is my time" she says. "No! No! No!" I resist. "It is not your time, Scott. You must be strong. For me. For the kids," she tells me. "I love you so much, Mary. I will always love you. You did good while you were here. You helped so many people," I cry. "I know," she says, "but thank you. It's OK for me to go now. My work here is done." "Don't go yet," I beg, "what will I do without you?" "You will find your path. And you will join me here. I will wait," she consoles. Lying on the beach alone, I have fallen on my own arms with my hands on my head, but right at this moment, I know it is Mary who is stroking my head, combing her fingers through my hair as she likes to do. I shudder through three total body-wracking spasms of despair as I realize she's leaving. She continues to stroke me. I calm down. I feel totally loved. "You must go now," she whispers, "I love you. I will help you with the kids. Don't worry. It's time. Go, sweetheart, go." "Goodbye, Mary Lou, I love you."

I stand up again. I feel so grateful for the chance to hug her, tell her I love her, and know she is OK for her journey. I feel exultant, alive. The beach seems lighter, the world a more positive, happier place. I meander around the beach, looking up, smiling. "What do you have in mind for me, universe?" I ask, "huh?" I pick up a small bit of beach glass where my head

was. Paces away I find my journal, where the rock missed me....
I am still standing!

Strolling back through the beach walk, I feel carefree, completely secure, fearless. I will teach. I am a teacher. "Teach Your Children" floods my mind. Crosby, Stills, Nash and Young. I always cry when I hear this old 60's song. Must learn the words now. Turning away from the path back to the condo, I wheel around the parking lot under the stars. I will teach. I will teach! "What will you teach me, universe?" So much to learn. "What is my truth?" My arms spread wide open to embrace the possibilities. The world is born anew for me. I will teach........

Chapter 16. "Goodbye Mary Lou"

It is January fourth, 2011, a gray day at the Cold Spring Harbor Library, where I sit to contemplate the five years since Mary's passing, and try to say, finally, farewell my beautiful Mary Lou. A lot has occurred in the intervening half decade, but much remains the same. I imagine her here with me, a vivacious 62 year old, restless, searching, struggling, smiling, touching everyone around her. It has been a tortuous journey for me, her children, and her closest family and friends. As much as Mary implored us to "move on, live the life you imagine, never let an adventure pass you by," it hasn't been that easy. I have hung on, reluctant to let go, recalcitrant to commit, timid to launch into a new era of my life, boldly, as she instructed. I am hopeful that writing this chapter in this book will allow me finally to turn the page....

The initial year of guilt over not connecting with Mary on the mountain as she was dying has lifted, thanks to her Jupiter, Florida intervention, but questions lingered about how she died. Do we know exactly how she was struck; did anyone see? No, but the most likely scenario is that an early rock, perhaps football size or less, struck her in the back before she could turn to face the onslaught. To my knowledge no one heard her cry out. Could she have been saved if better medical care was available? No. Her right lung was filling rapidly –the autopsy revealed two liters of blood in the lung. My best friend, Dr. Frederick Sherman, later commented that in his opinion "had this happened at the front door of one of the finest New York City hospitals, Mary still could not have been saved." How long did she live after being hit? Lucy from New Jersey, who walked down the Western Breach close to Mary's tarp-bearers, said later she died within a half hour of being struck, which would mean perhaps 15 minutes into the journey down the mountain. So, Mary's suffering was limited, at least in duration.

If there was a hero in our story, it was Kambona. His deft handling of the emergencies in the most difficult of circumstances is testimony to his experience, cool-headedness and unshakable character. Kambona is clearly someone one would want in a foxhole should a firefight break out. He was deeply moved by the disaster, took a brief respite, and has resumed leading groups up to the "Roof of Africa" on Mount Kilimanjaro. We stayed in contact with our fellow climbers for the first few months and saw Bill and Lucy on a few occasions that first year. They are all warm, welcoming people, but our reluctance, most particularly the children's aversion, to revisit the tragedy has kept us from staying close. A shame.

The children and I developed distinctly different methods of coping with what happened to us, and it meant early estrangement. Our visit to Bill and Lucy's house in Ridgewood, NJ in spring of '06 provided a perfect illustration. My approach to the tragedy was to explore, share, listen and try to understand, as a way to grasp the horror in a group way. During our blow-by-blow post mortem discussion of the fateful day's events in Bill and Lucy's living room, Trevor, Becky and John were quiet, stone-faced, as I participated whole-heartedly. In the car on the way home to Huntington after the meeting, Becky choked out she never wanted to endure that again. "It felt like someone was standing on my chest," she croaked. John and Trevor quickly echoed. I apologized. They needed to avoid "going back there," preferring to work it out individually and privately. I respected their wishes. I craved a way for the four of us to share our recollections and cry and absorb the event together, to get our collective arms around it. That was not in the cards.

Trevor, John and Becky have picked up the pieces in their own unique ways and are pursuing the life they are imagining. Ever the strong one, Trevor practices Zen and utilizes his intellect to navigate the sometimes choppy emotional waters. After two unfulfilling jobs in offices where he felt there was too much compromising to do, he has embarked on a freelance internet software teaching career. He travels from Orlando, Florida to Boston, Massachusetts, even including Dubai in the Middle East, and finds himself in the thick of the fast-moving development of internet commerce.

John has overcome a lackluster High School experience, received inspiration from his uncle Herb Sigmond, a member of Doctors Without Borders, and his harrowing trauma on Kilimanjaro, and caught fire in his crusade to become an Emergency Room doctor "anywhere the world needs me." He has an even-odds chance, as I write this, of achieving a 4.0 grade average in his penultimate semester of pre-med studies at SUNY Stony Brook. John's relentless pursuit of his dream has sustained him through the inevitable periods of self-doubt and overwhelmed feelings, not to mention the recurring sadness of losing his mom.

Becky carries the heaviest burden of loss after Mary's passing on Mount Kilimanjaro. In the interim she has been busy. She has published an article on evolutionary biology with a professor at SUNY Albany, launched a business selling soccer outerwear, videotaped and produced a dozen or more short documentaries for businesses, charities, a Galapagos tour operator, and families, traveled on her own to Guatemala and Ecuador, and worked in the film Department of CW Post College on Long Island. Her latest project is a book describing her relationship with her mom intertwined with the Kilimanjaro experience. We have been working in parallel, but separately. Her heart-felt wisdom shines through her writing.

Dee Margolis and Matt Viemeister have been bulwarks for me this last half decade, helping me through two more passings after Mary died on Kilimanjaro. Dee was very nervous about my experience on the beach in Jupiter, Florida in February 2007 – she felt the downside risk was so pronounced – but ultimately delighted and amazed I was able to renegotiate the trauma of Mary's passing on the mountain and absorb "how I would have acted, had circumstances allowed." After that catharsis, we were both quickly swept up in the oncoming cancer death of my iconic father Quentin in August of 2007, and the emotional aftermath. Following that we made our way through the death of my family business. I sold the business Quentin, Frank and I had built for 20 years together to what turned out to be a private equity company owned by Goldman Sachs. My naïve dreams of continued growth and opportunity succumbed to the wrecking ball of profit growth and "reductions in force." Soon after I retired in April, 2010, only 13 employees remained of the original 52 who were there when the business changed hands. It was a slow, relentless process of dying, and each layoff killed me a little too. I remember vividly working with Dee and Matt to dissipate my anger and sadness at each wave of layoffs and cutbacks. I will never be able to thank them enough for their strength, wisdom and guidance.

When I left the beach parking lot on A1A in Jupiter, Florida I was walking on air, moved by the possibility of these "impossible" conversations with Mary. I returned to my father's condo in the near-dawn light and scribbled furiously, capturing all the dialogue and plot as accurately as I could. My senses were all heightened, my memory was crystal clear. I believe I have the experience 99% correct. When I was first in contact with Mary through Jim Fargiono on July 12, 2006 she cautioned me that I would never be able to be aware of her presence. I kept myself open to the possibility anyway. I visit Jim every eleven months or so and Mary is completely present, ebullient, saucy, hilarious, and poignant. In the last five years I was only able to record one conversation that occurred without Jim's intervention. It took place in the early, pre-waking hours of a Sunday morning in June 2008. As soon as I awoke fully I transcribed it exactly:

Scott: "Were we soul mates?

Mary: "Yes."

Scott: "Are there others where you are?"

Mary: "It's different here. Strong, warm, special bonds, but with many souls. There is no sex like humans have, but much more ecstatic connections, all the time. We are all connected, without the human worries and pettiness."

Scott: "Can I be a soul mate to another woman?"

Mary: "Yes. You can have several. I am not there with you, so, yes you can."

Scott: "When I'm there with you and so is she?"

Mary (laughs): "Stop worrying. There is no jealousy or possessiveness here - it's a human, earthly thing. We got over it."

Scott: "Why were you restless, searching?"

Mary: "Problems from my childhood I never quite figured out. I thought if I went back to California I could recapture what I'd lost. I didn't know I could have it wherever I was. You offered me completely adoring love and I rejected it. My mistake. I didn't figure it out until too late, and I made you pay. I'm so sorry. So sorry. You could have given me what I needed. I was close to figuring it out through all my therapies, and, had Mount Kilimanjaro not happened, I would have."

Scott: "Would we have made it, without Mount

Kilimanjaro?"

Mary: "Yes. I would have gotten it. I would have let my guard and worries down, learned to let you love me, and got my sex drive back. We would have made love everywhere, shocking and delighting my girlfriends. Even in a coat closet at a fundraiser. You would have been in HEAVEN."

Scott: "What about your independence?

Mary: "The more time I spent away from you, the deeper I loved and appreciated you. You didn't see that? Dummy."

Scott: "Did you have an affair?"

Mary; "No. Some 'stolen kisses' like I said, but never sealed the deal. Didn't want to hurt you and the kids. Don't ask who, I'm not telling. Not important.

Scott: "O.K."

Mary: "I realize my role in driving you to your affair and how you resisted. You were weak, I was cold. I would have forgiven you 100% if Mount Kilimanjaro didn't happen."

Scott: "Was I wrong not to come to you on Mount Kilimanjaro?"

Mary: "No. The thought that your soul mate was close to death was too big and awful to deal with. You loved me too much. And you do live in a fantasy world sometimes. Your kids were with me, and the guys. You did fine. I'm glad I could straighten you out at Jupiter Beach." (smile, kiss)

Scott: "How's Quentin doing?"

Mary: "Interesting to see him with his dad. They are building a better, stronger bond, with love replacing jealousy, suspicion and distrust."

Scott: "What about the estate?"

Mary: "He has strong ideas – from his dad and one other guy – that giving too much spoils children. You could not have changed his mind. I know I asked you to, but it wasn't going to happen. It's just Quentin, that's all."

Scott: "Should I bring Marge to Jim?"

Mary: "Yes. Quentin needs to talk to her. It's the right thing."

Scott: "Should I have sold the business if you didn't leave?"

Mary: "Yes. We'd be discussing how to go enjoy the money. That would have made me happy and secure."

Scott: "Would I have worked the next three years?"

Mary: "Yes, to make sure you got the rest of the money. I was champing at the bit, went on some trips myself, but we got through it. It was going to be a wonderful life – and a long one."

Scott: "Would you get Alzheimer's?"

Mary: "Yes, but much later, and they developed great drugs for it. I died before you, but not by much. We had a TON of fun. Not a terrible death. Lots of love around me."

Scott: "What should I do next?"

Mary: "I said 'teach,' but more broadly I mean, use your words to reach people, connect to their hearts, show them your philosophy, help them find strength and peace. You have a great gift for this. Use your words. The money will come. You'll see. Don't worry so much. There is a vast reservoir of love and peace and calm among humanity. You need to tap into it and spread it. You need never feel alone."

Scott: "The kids?"

Mary: "Marvelous. I'm so proud of them all I can't believe it. You are a perfect support, platform, guide, advisor, etc. who can give them the freedom to pursue what they love. They are all becoming great adults. You must be proud also. Love them with all your heart."

Scott: "I do."

Mary: "You must let the world love you. Let them love you. They want to. And go easy on religion. There is more good than bad in it. Smarter people will figure out the charade, and the weaker will only become more panicky and depressed. Most of it is man-made and there are abuses, no doubt. But, go easy. Let the world love you. Like I love you."

As I retell this heartwarming conversation with Mary, the sun has come out in Cold Spring Harbor. My spirits are lifting, It is time for the finale. Have I become a teacher? Maybe, with this book, yes. Some lessons from my life with Mary are here.

If one young couple can stop placing bricks in the invisible emotional wall between them and find a way not to burn down their marriage, then Mary and I will have become teachers, and succeeded.

This last section is a sensitive one. In the hotel in Arusha, Mary urged me to move on, to be happy. In the session with Jim Fargiono that first summer after she died, she exculpated me, reassured me and gave me permission to find another love. Here, 30 months after she passed, she found me in a semi-conscious dreamlike place and made it easy for me to go forward romantically and be loved again. Each time I believed it in my head, but my heart couldn't let go. I am clearly "the marrying kind," my friends will tell you. I need to be needed and I need to take care of a partner as well. I want a best friend, confidante, and soul mate. Some folks believe "soul mate" is a foolish, unattainable fictional product of Hollywood, but I am a hopeful romantic. I had a wonderful 30 year relationship with Mary, replete with rocky periods, but on balance delightful. I knew another one could happen. I held out hope and tried several times in the years since Mary passed. It began to seem like it wasn't going to happen for me. Maybe I should settle for a comfortable, manageable relationship....

Over the past 5 years a few wonderful females have volunteered to try to make another 30 year honeymoon happen with me. They did nothing wrong. Early in each attempt, right after the initial giddy, bubble time, the real world would intrude. She would say things like "let's go meet my family, attend a wedding, go to a birthday party for my nephew, etc." I would break out in a sweat, become morose, and run for the exit. "Check please," I would hear myself saying in my own head. The ladies were frustrated, I'm sure, but they were perceptive, also. They knew, in their heart of hearts, I wasn't available. I still loved Mary and clung to her memory. Maybe by "replacing her," I thought I would lose her? I was reluctant to introduce my dates to my children, so I kept my dating under the radar. Did I not want to upset the children with the prospect of replacing their mom? Did I fear their disapproval? Who knows.

In the latter half of this half decade I was able to come

closest to commitment with a strong, independent woman with whom I shared several common interests. She was extricating herself from a long marriage, for her own private reasons. Married for over 60% of her entire life, she didn't need me to marry her, or promise to. We enjoyed our interests, including cross-country motorcycling, and became best friends. I didn't need to commit completely, and that was a good thing, because I couldn't have at that point in my life. Looking back, I was simply unable. Had she demanded more of me I know I would have panicked and run. I suspect she was not ready for more either. Our break up was painful, because we cared a lot for each other. We remain friends.

I now believe my ability to write this book, or inability, over the past five years parallels my readiness, or recalcitrance, to commit to a new 30 year romance. The idea of writing Goodbye Mary Lou has been with me since the month Mary died on the mountain. That January I entertained the thought of convening a gathering of many of her relatives and friends to bring together stories of Mary's life and collect them for a tribute book. I quickly realized I was in no way emotionally equipped to face all of that and scuttled the plan.

Eighteen months after she died I tried again, pulling out my journals and feeling the emotions all over again. This proved much too depressing and arduous. Dee said "stop, why are you torturing yourself? Do something fun, take it easy this summer, why don't you try Match.com?" I tried Match for two weeks and enjoyed the two week distraction. The book would have to wait. I simply wasn't ready.

By the summer of 2010 Becky said she was writing about her special connection to Mary in the months before she died. She was weaving together a tapestry of vignettes, anecdotes and stories with her narrative of the Kilimanjaro saga. I was inspired and touched. I began my writing again. By the time September rolled around I had 45 pages produced and was enthused with the emotional process. Instead of the sad heaviness, I felt a lightness, a joy at unburdening, sharing, expressing these thoughts.

As the writing process was gathering momentum that late summer, I received a phone call from a delightful lady I had worked with briefly two years earlier. Her name was Tina. I'd felt a strong attraction for her back then, but never mentioned it to anyone until we stopped working together. We saw each other in business venues in the next few months, and I thought I saw a look in her eyes that indicated interest. She was trying to make her marriage work so I turned away. Six months passed. This phone call was to inform me her marriage was unsalvageable, and would I like to have dinner? I cannot explain the euphoria that suffused me. I felt something stir within me. Hope, maybe. I remembered how I felt when I was with Tina – I hadn't felt this way since my early days with Mary, so completely comfortable, warm and relaxed. I wondered if I couldn't have another 30 year honeymoon with Tina. Was it possible?

During the summer of 2010 I had struggled to understand what was missing in my current relationship. There was warmth and connection and the common interests, but there was also frustration, distance, and bickering. My children noticed my uneasiness, bordering on unhappiness, and called for a family meeting, also known as an intervention. "Dad," they said, "you don't sound happy to us. We all want one thing – your happiness. You have been saying recently you've begun to think that asking the universe for a new soul mate like Mom is asking too much. We've heard you say 'most folks don't even get ONE soul mate in a lifetime. Asking for a second one seems selfish, even piggy. I should probably just settle for a comfortable, low maintenance relationship and be as happy as I can be.' To us, Dad, that idea is utter bullshit! You keep looking. Don't you stop until you find the love of your life. You need it, you deserve it, and so do we. Don't you dare give up." Wow, I thought as the tears filled my eyes, "I've just been ambushed by Mary's posse of Dutch Uncles."

When the call came from Tina and the dinner happened, I was overwhelmed with emotion. Were Mary and the kids right? Was my second chance right here in front of me? If so, I 'd better go for it. The last few months have been a whirlwind. We have fallen head over heels in love. You can spot us everywhere. We are the couple with the look in their eyes that Tina calls "the bakery face look." You know, the look that people get when they first smell that fresh baked bread or chocolate chip cookie: dazed surrender to the pleasure of the moment. Simultaneously I have relentlessly written these chapters. The bulk were produced in eight days in Key West, Florida, where I channeled my inner Hemingway. We have plans to be married in the near future and I couldn't be happier.

Mary, I love you, and I will never forget you. I know you loved me. I am following your wishes, finally, and moving on. I will set an example for our children. By being as happy as I can, and loving Tina with 100% of my energy, I am honoring you, your life, your lessons, and your legacy. Goodbye, my sweet Mary Lou.

The real saying goodbye is in the writing of this book. I have dissolved into tears 40+ times as the emotions poured out, once again. I feel one door closing and one door opening. Goodbye, Mary Lou, Hello Tina. Do you ever really say goodbye to someone as important in your life as Mary Lou was to me? No. It's more like "farewell, I will never forget you." But, for five years I worried. Maybe the power and poignancy and the need and love of our marriage would fade over time, slip away into the mists of failing human memory. Now, they cannot. Mary's story is permanent, not subject to the frail vagaries of memory. Now the details can never slip away. They are here, on paper and in bytes, for me, for Mary Lou, and for you, dear reader. Goodbye, Mary Lou.

www.ingramcontent.com/pod-product-compliance
Lightning Source LLC
Chambersburg PA
CBHW071407120626
46546CB00002B/847